P9-CEQ-809

Board Life

Also by ROBERT KIRK MUELLER

Effective Management Through Probability Controls
Risk, Survival, and Power
The Innovation Ethic
Buzzwords

Board
Life

Realities of Being a
Corporate Director

Robert Kirk Mueller

Illustrated by Ric Estrada

A Division of American Management Associations

Any resemblance to actual board life situations or to directors, living or dead, is strictly coincidental, fortunate or unfortunate. If a director fancies he recognizes himself or others, the author disclaims any responsibility.

Appreciation of their tutelage and their wisdom is hereby expressed to many colleagues with whom the author has been privileged to serve.

© 1974 AMACOM
A division of American Management Associations, New York.
All rights reserved. Printed in the United States of America.

This publication may not be reproduced, stored in a retrieval system, or transmitted in whole or in part, in any form or by any means, electronic, mechanical, photocopying, recording, or otherwise, without the prior written permission of AMACOM.

International standard book number: 0-8144-5346-5
Library of Congress catalog card number: 73-85190

First printing

Preface

In the mid-fifties, when labor and public sympathy with labor relations crises dominated boardrooms more than they do now, I was asked by a close friend, board member, and senior officer of a *Fortune* 500 firm to join a Vice-Presidents' Union. This invitation was partly in jest, for the organization was strictly a calling-card creation, but it leveled a protesting needle at the establishment's painful preoccupation with organized labor's demands for improvement in the quality of life and particularly the time spent away from work and off the job. Furthermore, the high priority then afforded personnel matters in the boardroom left relatively neglected the situation of top managers and directors themselves. The contested focus was entirely on vacations, pensions, coffee breaks, health and hospitalization plans, and holidays. To a scattering of officers in several industrial firms this misdirected emphasis seemed to constitute inordinate attention to the wrong part of the problem.

How to make the time devoted to all tasks more rewarding, pleasant, and stimulating appeared to be a better perspective, whether the job was in a boiler room or a boardroom. The work–time ambiance of factory, laboratory, executive suite, and boardroom was believed to be more in need of attention.

The Vice-Presidents' Union lasted for about a year, until executive mobility broke up the VPU order. We all went about our respective careers in top management and directorates with the feeling that occasionally some thought to the individual's viewpoint was a good thing and that an organized "labor" approach to improving a corporate situation—albeit misdirected according to certain points of view—should not always be suspect, as is often the case at the officer or director level. Such endeavors sometimes provoke us to think in fruitful directions. Our union met only randomly, when two or three of us came together in the course of business, but the concept of looking after one's personal future and value judgments in the framework of an institutionalized milieu is still a relatively damped phenomenon —at least at many directorate levels.

Now, in the early seventies, public, employee, and government attention to the social responsibility of business has put this worrisome concern at the top of boardroom agendas and raised its priority in the executive suite. Shareowners, minority groups, environmentalists, conservationists, regulatory agencies, the Justice Department, and various public interest organizations are challenging the performance of top management and particularly the performance of the board of directors. We are asked, "Who is business's keeper?" Well-publicized charges against managements and directorates run the gamut from immorality, self-perpetuating oligarchy, conflicts of interest, and insider dealings to environmental and consumer insensitivity. Pressure is increasing to change certain practices and concepts.

The Securities and Exchange Commission has proposed codes of ethics which, among other things, require that directors of investment companies file reports on personal securities transactions. The Federal Trade Commission's landmark action in 1972 against interlocking directorates in the case against Alcoa, Kennecott, and Armco extends the Clayton Act into a new area, the objective of which is to fix responsibility on the corporation for the elimination of interlocks. Sir Frederick Snow has suggested that Britain's Institute of Directors obtain a Royal

Charter which would entitle the organization to audit qualifications and performance and use the descriptive term "chartered
directors." The Watkinson Committee of the Bank of England
and the Confederation of British Industry have proposed a much
tougher code of practices for British boards of directors.

This escalation of concern from trade and professional
groups, consumers, government, and the public at large spot-
lights the need for dramatically improved board effectiveness
and significant changes in board practice. While measures aimed
at strict conformity are not warranted, some aspects of boardroom affairs and practice really do need attention in order that
boards can respond to the future challenges of their function.
Laws and regulations are being tightened around the world to
effect better performance and to clarify accountability and responsibility. The literature containing accounting, legal, ethical,
and organizational advice to directors is accumulating. But in
the main these caveats, no-no's, exhortations, liabilities, constraints, and penalties are offered from the viewpoint of the
public, the shareowner, the management, the government, and
the directorate itself.

Little if any guidance in a pragmatic sense is available
to the aspirant director who, undaunted by the rising uncertainties of responsibility and liabilities of directors these days,
still seeks the flycast invitation to stand for election as a director.
A constant-companion handbook—*vade mecum*—is needed for
the real work and affairs of the director. This book is only a
start in that direction and is offered from experience more as a
descriptive than a prescriptive guide. The would-be director
will have to interpret some of the more sensitive areas herein as
judiciously as possible. He had better seek professional counsel,
however, if he is at all uncomfortable about certain of the practices he may be exposed to or expected to participate in. He
also needs to carefully review the technical requirements of
being a director and to keep up to date on legal, tax, and accounting interpretations of such activities.

A starter bibliography at the end of the book contains
sources of real technical know-how that envelops the director
function. Supplementing this, of course, are the various tax,
investment, business policy, and legal service reports which are

available from private and public professional sources. With such a wealth of professional literature available, no attempt is made in this handbook of boardroom behavior (as I see it) to provide expert advice to *Americanus commitatus,* which is Harvard Professor Emeritus M. L. Mace's term for these business "birds"—the various species of directors.

The responsibility is strictly mine for any insight (or oversight) into the behavior and affairs of director species, their care and feeding. Equally important to such sole responsibility for this *vade mecum* is the tribute due my fellow directors and professionals who have shared some of these perspectives and scenarios with me or who have coached me on the diverse and intriguing sidelights and delights of directorships. These colleagues could each have written such a guide from their own experience, and undoubtedly their insights would be somewhat different. As James Russell Lowell said, "Truly there is a tide in the affairs of men, but there is no gulf-stream setting forever in one direction."

Robert Kirk Mueller

Foreword

If you are able to think about the tail of a cat without thinking concurrently about the cat to which it is attached, then you are able to enjoy the usual writings about boards of directors. For most writers on the subject fail to recognize that the corporate board of directors is an institution that is merely part of a larger changing institution. As a part of the corporate enterprise, the board should be an appropriate extension of the reality of its particular corporation and also of the expectations that society from time to time has for all corporations. When corporations were regarded by their managers and by society generally as purely economic machinery to maximize profits, it would have been absurd to discuss board composition in terms of women, blacks, consumers, or workers. Today it is absurd not to do so.

The great value of Robert Kirk Mueller's analysis is that he sets the institution of the board of directors in its corporate and social contexts. He cuts through myth, not grimly with a dull mace, but with a keen scalpel and a sense of history, of sociology, and of humor. In dissecting the tail of the corporate cat, he remembers—unlike so many other corporate surgeons—not only that he is analyzing part of a whole but also that he is analyzing a lesser part. Some may dispute my analogy and argue that the board of directors is at the head, not at the tail. I would not disagree in every specific case, for, as Mueller points out, each boardroom is a changing institution within a changing corporate institution within a changing society.

Since the author has been an inside director, outside director, statutory director, honorary director, advisory director, multinational director, and surrogate director at various times and on various kinds of boards—for profit, service and manufacturing, trade association and professional society boards—he knows well the territory his guidebook covers. There is a feel for the reality of the marketplace as well as the scholarship of the library. But not dry fact and dusty learning. Throughout the carefully assembled data and wealth of hardheaded advice, there percolates a delightful, lighthearted stream of anecdotes and observations.

My own boardroom experiences include fisticuffs between two directors, a summons served on the directorate by what we took to be a waiter bringing coffee, and a somewhat senile chap who was regularly led to the boardroom table by an attendant. This last gentleman once bestirred himself to argue that we should call the preferred stock, since the dividend was not tax deductible. The board members were well into a spirited debate before someone pointed out that the preferred had been called many years before most of us joined the board. Thereupon one dissenting director cursed out the chairman and demanded that the minutes record his four-letter vocabulary. On the other hand, I have attended board meetings of great complexity and dead seriousness when soul-searching decisions had to be made on removal of management, instituting major litigation, and risking much of the net worth on a new venture.

Anyone who has spent many hours in boardrooms will confirm that Mueller has seen what it is like and tells it as it is.

Let me offer only four bits of advice to the novice director reading this handbook:

1 Avoid joining boards composed of people whose occupation is attending meetings. You will be the only one with a desire to adjourn. Nonprofit boards composed of ministers, social workers, and housewives are

hazardous, but also beware of corporate boards composed only of retirees.

2 Withdraw from boards where the principal executive does not occasionally provide easy social contact with different levels of management. Most outside directors who have been caught in corporate scandals would have been alerted by some members of lower management if they had been reasonably accessible to each other.

3 Treat your director compensation as found money to be spent on extravagances and charities. Then you'll never have financial reasons for hesitating to dissent or resign.

4 Occasionally reread this book. Not only is it delightful, perceptive, and comprehensive—but there is much wisdom that you will appreciate more after having had boardroom experience of your own.

Eli Goldston
Chairman, Eastern Gas and Fuel Associates
Boston, Massachusetts

Contents

1 The Determinative Society

What some folks are born in, others are taken in, but most folks pay to get in.

There always has been snob appeal about regents, viziers, governors, trustees, directors, and other actors on the stage of leadership. If you are not a director, chances are that you strive to be one, and you'd like to have your daughter marry into such circles or capture a threshold candidate. Also, if you are not a pacesetter in this determinative society, you probably conceal the fact and take every opportunity to associate with those who are. Most of us reserve some awe for those who are institutionally anointed as members of so sacrosanct a society as the directorates.

If you happen to enjoy such enshrinement, you make sure others know of it, especially when they are from another country, another industry, or another field of endeavor. This forestalls ready comparisons of the true significance of your stewardship. It also feeds the mythical value systems which endow character and status to the determinative boards of domestic and foreign institutions.

The eliteness motivation is a particular stirring force in the business world, which has its own extension ladders into this attic of the conventional business hierarchy. Almost axiomatic in a business institution, the progression from manager to officer to director, the unquestioned step-up of chief executive officer to the position of chairman of the board, all fail to face up to the real determinative function of the directorate. Like professional societies, the military, or the church, a lemming-like progression of insider administrators to trustee positions is part of this established business society system. Normal practices and organizational conventions tend to preserve the system and the directors' own future by tacit predetermined selection of director majorities. The system then generally employs a subtle enriching "care and feeding" program to keep the individual directors fat, happy, and relatively contained.

Only recently has this self-serving societal setup been challenged by the shareholder, the consumer, the customer, the supplier, the employee, the public, and, healthily, in some instances the managers or directors themselves. As a result, directorates and directors are caught in the cross fire. Increasing potential liability and restraints on directors' freedom of action make this determinative society feel persecuted at times. In late January 1972 discharged workers who were striking over a wage dispute at a factory in San Sebastian, Spain, kidnapped the chairman of the board and held him hostage until the board rehired the workers and guaranteed a $15 per month wage increase. The chairman was released unharmed after the extortion. While extortion is one of the rarer hazards that directors face, increasing liabilities of all sorts have caused some fallout that has tarnished the tinsel adorning the directorate.

Despite such pressures the boardroom remains a pinnacle of achievement to many and always will. This is good, for the conditions of membership in this society are toughening in everyone's long-term interest. Regardless of the motivation, it is redeeming, then, that aspirations to become directors continue to be whetted.

In addition to attracting candidates to its directorate, the corporate body—a person in the juristic sense—has certain internal resources with which to deal with its responsibilities. The board of directors is a key resource and is the focus of the corporation's determinative powers. The directorate acts as the brain of the institution. Management literature is explicit about certain of these brainy functions, such as decision-making powers, legal obligations, and responsibilities of boards and their members. But public concern has recently questioned the determinative "mind" of the directorate in other legal, intellectual, and economic matters such as political, cultural, and environmental impact. The determinative "soul" of the directorate is also up for review, with the focus on its ethical and moral attitudes toward the society which sanctions its existence.

While consideration grows over the mind and soul of the board, little has been said as to the "heart" of the board in its concern about the internal and external relationships of the directorate as an entity and of the directors as individuals. Nowhere do we hear "second to the e-motion" in board matters, yet in many instances it is human complications at the board level that cause the rise and fall of institutions. The analogy should not be carried much further, although who is there to say that most boards do not have a derriere! Too often the directorate body succumbs to that well-known director's disease subanococcygeal plumbism—a disease debilitating to the determinative society.

Boardroom and Board

Public opinion cloaks a board of directors in an aura of sanctity which, some people say, approaches that of the College of Cardinals. Boardrooms appear altogether inaccessible. The reason is that the law sees a board as its members depict themselves: staunch, stern guardians of the shareholders' rights in the institution's long-term future.

The board nominates itself, in essence elects itself, and then congratulates itself as a self-perpetuating oligarchy. Directors are supposed to hold management accountable for performance, but often this discipline is slow acting if it acts at all. The disciplining of managers may have been effective when top managers were not members of the board. Today the president or managing director is likely to be the chief executive officer or even the chairman of the board, and—understandably—he identifies himself primarily with the upper group of management and the board rather than with the shareholders. This clique of top management raises some unresolved issues about relationships between the directors, the management, the shareholders, and the company itself. As Robert Heller notes, the dominance of the board is perhaps "less Sicilian" in the United States than it is in some European and Far Eastern organizations. But the outcome is essentially the same: too few corporations have a real check and balance performed by the separate function of the board as distinct from the management or by the chairman as distinct from the chief executive officer.

The concept of having the chief executive function one step down from the board, as a check and balance, has certain virtues. There is an obvious tangle in the historical relationship of the executive chairman or the president and his colleagues in management, their interdependence, and the hierarchical relationship of the president and, say, his vice presidents. For a vice president–director to challenge his president's policies at board level is too much to ask of a fellow unless he has a vested pension and an outside income.

The statutory activity of the board and the rain dance which is necessary from ceremonial and obligations standpoints frequently take up an inordinate amount of time and prevent the board from facing the basic issues where a true check and balance should be exercised. The insider-dominated board as a judicial body reigning over the management is O.K. in theory, but with few exceptions, actual practice is another thing. There are unwritten laws or propositions between inside directors and management, such that seldom do they challenge each other at the trustee level. Otherwise, conflict comes out in the open. This exposes a lack of directorate coherence, which in itself is difficult to deal with. Critical issues are not often exposed by an individual director unless he is willing to risk damage to his own career in pressing a basic controversy with his superiors in management who are his peers on the board. Thus the conventional board tends to be self-protective, self-perpetuating, and too involved in the cult of personality of the leader or in the lack of such leadership.

An inside director cannot be truly objective about judging his own proposals when it comes to allocating corporate resources for his proposed project or for a project sponsored by another inside director. With some noteworthy exceptions, too many boards face this possibility because they have a dominant inside board with no realistic check from outsiders. The disadvantage of outsiders is that they may not be familiar enough with the business, but this is no reason to eliminate a check and balance between board and management. Companies like Texas Instruments have pioneered in correcting this fault (see Chapter 4).

While a board is, in theory, designed to guarantee that vested interests don't jeopardize the interests of the company as a whole, in practice it doesn't always work that way. Non-executive or outside directors, no matter how able and informed, are seldom in a position to question the integrity and judgment of a senior managerial group that is proposing a major project. No outside director can match the staff work involved; at best he can insist on thorough staff work on alternates. Thus some non-executive directors tend to be only ornamental, or they serve as bridges with the legal fraternity, the accounting fraternity, and financial organizations. These directorial links provide important outside perspective but present other problems, as we shall see.

Determinative Effectiveness

The pressures to improve the effectiveness of the board of directors usually focus on the chairman or chief executive officer, who is expected to take the initiative in thinking through the functions of the board and in proposing new structures, relationships, and actions for this determinative body. One president uses a "mushroom strategy" in his dealings with his board of directors: "Keep 'em in the dark and feed 'em lots of manure." He expresses it a bit less elegantly, but it does convey the not uncommon practice of keeping the directors at arm's length and feeding them a management formula which may or may not be objective. Such a relationship is truly out of date.

Directors themselves are becoming more aware of their legal obligations and liabilities and are asking for greater participation in corporate determinative affairs, including new forms of compensation, indemnification, and protection. This is causing a rethink on the actions of boards and their relationship with the management with particular emphasis on defining the director–management relationship.

A 1972 study by H. R. Land & Company, management consultants, on 60 U.S. corporations active in all segments of the economy reveals some noteworthy aspects to this new concern for boardroom effectiveness. The survey sample included small privately owned firms and medium-size regionally traded companies as well as widely traded *Fortune* 500 corporations. The

The board was a mirror image of the CEO's desires and intentions.

findings revealed that more often than not the principal determinant of the effectiveness of a board of directors is the chief executive officer (CEO). In many situations he also acts as chairman of the board. The survey of these 60 corporations showed that the CEO's personal convictions as to what a board should be will do more to shape the role of the directors than any other single factor. In most instances the survey found that the board was a mirror image of the CEO's desires and intentions. There were exceptions, of course, particularly where individuals represented major equity interests or financial institutions that were not necessarily of the chief executive's choosing.

It was pointed out that the attitude of the CEO is critical, for he alone can create the atmosphere of candor and frankness in which the directors feel that their participation is of real value. While friendship plays a part, the relationship must remain a business rather than a personal one if the directorate is to perform a check and balance function with regard to the management. The survey revealed that the most effective boards seemed to share a philosophy in which the CEO and the directors consider themselves donors and recipients, a mutually beneficial relationship.

The effort of the CEO to select, attract, involve, motivate, compensate, and protect his directors is really a personal matter and depends a great deal on personal touches: private

A director is like a woman—he must be constantly wooed.

meetings, lunches, being aware of the personal and business obligations of each director. One prominent director was quoted as saying, "A director is like a woman—he must be constantly wooed." The care and feeding of directors can be a full-time job for the chairman or CEO if he lets it be. Sex and the single director, however, are beyond the scope of this book.

The Land study revealed eight criteria useful in picking an effective director:

1 Does he have broad experience with general management problems?
2 Is he a good listener who is not afraid to speak his mind?
3 Does he have sufficient time available?
4 Potentially, how great is his interest?
5 Is he free from the *cloud* of potential conflict of interest?
6 Is he compatible with management and the other directors?
7 Is his stature at least equal to that of the other directors?
8 Does he have a unique contribution to make?

The survey uncovered a series of questions around their own circumstances and those of the corporation which candidate directors pondered before accepting an invitation to stand for election. From a personal standpoint, the eight major questions were along the following lines:

1 Do I have adequate time available?
2 What effect would accepting have on my career?
3 How would my job and my company be affected?
4 What personal gain would accrue from this opportunity?
5 Do I respect management, its policies and direction?
6 Is the company financially sound?
7 Does the firm have a good reputation?
8 Am I compatible with management and the other directors?

The chief forces motivating an individual director were the potential personal relationships with other directors and with management, the satisfaction attendant upon board membership, and the status and prestige attached to the directorship. Fees and retainers were rarely cited, although the opportunity for a capital gain is a strong motivating factor.

The survey pointed out that the key to making a director effective is to involve him personally in the company affairs, to tailor-make the focus for each individual director so that he can contribute. Keeping directors informed by phone and mail, having them attend certain management meetings, including their wives where appropriate, and arranging selective business trips are simple tactics to accomplish this.

The survey revealed practical, if obvious, suggestions as to how to organize activities to make board meetings more effective. Providing board books that are divided into two major sections was suggested, with a current section for material pertinent to the next meeting and a permanent section for information to be used on a continuing basis. Delivering the board book a week before the scheduled meeting and collecting it at the end of the session is the usual practice. This keeps the directors well informed, allows the chief executive to focus the board meeting, and gives the directors time to do their homework.

Typical items included in the current section of the board book were agenda, minutes of the previous meetings, reports of the president and the financial officer, any adjustments to the plan, issues to be voted on, and policy issues or presentations by management. Typical items included in the permanent section of the board book were board meeting schedule, committee membership of the board, corporate structure, organization charts, names and addresses of directors, financial history on a ten-year financial basis similar to that included in the annual report, annual plan, graphic presentations of corporate performance, articles and bylaws, promotional materials, and current annual and quarterly reports.

As far as director compensation is concerned, most chief executives contacted in the survey believed that a director's compensation should approximately equal what he would receive for an equivalent amount of time spent in his own profession. Others judge the appropriateness of director compensation by comparing it to what a professional management consultant with equivalent background and experience would receive. The usual form is annual retainers, recognizing the constant availability of the director beyond the meetings he attends. One of the revealing findings of the survey was that many directors consider themselves undercompensated, given the responsibility and liability they have assumed. An innovative new trend in director compensation appears to be the cafeteria approach. Here the CEO sits down with each board member, gives him the general compensation parameters, then allows the director to choose the forms of compensation most meaningful to him. As in a cafeteria, the possibilities are many and varied: cash, capital gains opportunities, insurance, automobiles, and other perquisites. The Land survey describes the legal obligations that directors are concerned about. Most directors look to management for protection in these matters. If a director lacks confidence in the chief executive officer, he usually declines the invitation to membership. Director and officer liability insurance is now carried by most firms at the request of board members.

Directorcraft

While much has been written and surveyed about the loftier aspects of the position of directors, not much has been said about the determinative factors at the skill or "craft" level in the boardroom. Skills and crafts are distinct from the more abstract talents of a professional director. Skills and craft capability imply those activities which you can, and do, do yourself. These are distinct from some professional practice, wherein you may be able to do something yourself, but you usually do it no longer because you can get others to do it for you. As a professional you observe their performance from a detached and objective perspective.

The importance of evaluating the acts of a director from a skills and craft viewpoint depends on what participation occurs at board meetings, how well a director does his homework, the number of sound questions he raises as well as the number of foolish or naïve questions he doesn't raise, and the outside practical input that he provides. In some cases, director input may be from a professional detached viewpoint; but if it is in the craft category, it should stem from his personal ability to judge rather than from something he has read or learned indirectly. Thus a banker on a board would employ his own bankcraft as a major input, and he would be listened to by the other members of the board as someone who knows what he is talking about because he "can do it himself." On the other hand, a banker or a lawyer talking about an area of emerging technology in which he is not expected to have expertise (even though he may be more advanced and open-minded than someone who is) doesn't have the same impact as an expert in the craft. The interdisciplinary dimension is valuable, of course, so both lines of inquiry or thought should be encouraged.

Director skills include social skill, intellectual skill, economic skill, political skill, and any functional skill such as marketing or manufacturing or accounting. Skills are valuable to an institution in that they can be tapped by the board to assist the enterprise or to check out something.

The determinative society—the board of directors—should be an elite corps with professional talents, special skills, and "crafts" available because of the great need for philosophical leadership, purpose, and directional decisions in most economic institutions. The director's task is formidable and never-ceasing. Defining purpose, maintaining identity, controlling destiny, and dealing with responsibility to the greater sovereign society that sanctions such establishments as a corporation is an exciting challenge. The more a candidate director can learn about the real-life practice of directors, the greater can be his effectiveness.

2 Welcome Aboard

A director is not the same as a confessor . . . a confessor hears avowals of sin, a director is consulted in "cases of conscience."

The French Constitution of 1795 established the Directory, which vested the executive function in five "directors," one of whom retired every year. After a sickly existence of four years, it came to an end at Napoleon's coup d'etat in 1799. The modern board is nowhere threatened out of existence like this French entity, nor is the French Directory by any means the earliest root of the directorate concept. Directorates have been traced to 2083 B.C., when the Babylonian Code of Hammurabi set forth a special type of long-life partnership through which business could be carried on for years. In ancient Rome the corporate form of *societates* required a board of directors to assume limited liabilities. The concept of the corporation was furthered as an artificial entity when created in the thirteenth century under the papal authority of Innocent IV. According to Professor Harold Koontz of the University of California at Los Angeles, the modern business board of directors traces its immediate ancestry to the early English joint stock company board of proprietors.

So election to a board of directors is in a time-honored tradition reaching into antiquity. The reason for the current challenges and threats to directorates is their widely varied effectiveness, or lack of it, in carrying out the basic function of a board of directors.

Why Be a Director?

For insiders, election to the board of directors is a source of power and prestige. For outsiders, the rationale is partly prestige, partly to get to know the men they respect who are already on the board, partly to get away from their own companies, and partly to hear others on problems similar to their own. Outsiders also accept board membership because they think they can serve usefully or meet an obligation to be of service. In the early days a person may have taken the position of director in order to get inside information, which, of course, is no longer legal.

There are also you-scratch-my-back, I-scratch-yours aspects to accepting a directorship, since in practice the chief executive who invites another to stand for election onto his board generally expects a reciprocal invitation to stand for election on the other's board. In some companies all directors work full time as directors and don't attempt to double in brass as officers. The justification for this practice varies with the size, philosophy, and tradition of the company.

In a social sense boards have far-reaching powers. By their approval or disapproval they direct the flow of capital, and they start new industries or businesses which sometimes drive out old ones. This is a very potent reason for wanting to be a director. Some of the strongest forces at work on a director, both positive and negative, are those that Professor John B. Miner of the University of Maryland has termed eliteness motivation. This involves rubbing shoulders with people you admire —an upward pressure from the standpoint of achievement—as well as the more mundane but important matters of cultural and educational background, personal style, personality, dress, manners, poise, and general state of maturity. What makes the public relations profile of the peer group most important to an individual is that he is associated with a star system employed by the institution. Having fellow stars on the board is another heady attraction. In one recent five-year period at least nine out of ten corporations in the United States elected one or more new outside directors. A typical board elects three or more directors every five years, so openings are constantly being created. Four out of five times, selection of directors comes from suggestions of the present directors or the management, according to studies on this practice. And nine times out of ten, the selection of an individual as a director is dependent on his business experience and business reputation.

The opportunity to contribute and the reputation of the company represent more than half the appeal that attracts an outside director to a corporation. Although the number is small, perhaps less than one corporation in ten, there is an increasing interest in professional directors. At least three-quarters of corporations evidence no interest in retired executives for directors; and in about three-quarters of all U.S. corporations, half the board is made up of outside directors.

Professional Directors

A description of professional directors as unique inhabitants of boardrooms is given in Chapter 4. But in the context of "Why be a director?" it is worthwhile to examine an area where professional directorship is particularly needed, and to be needed is one reason for wanting to respond in a director role. The qualifications of a professional director are high, but so are the needs that can be satisfied in the system.

For the person interested in the unique value of a professional director, there appear to be at least six prospective and growing market needs for this breed.

1. The chief executive officer needs, without commitment, open dialog and interchange of ideas on his problems, plans, and dreams. Too frequently this dialog is not possible or appropriate with his captive staff or with his captive and regular directors. If perchance such dialog is possible with his regular associates, true objectivity and originality are unlikely because of the inherent obligations of insiders or captive board members. An outside professional director can insure the availability of unbiased counsel.

2. The chairman of the board, if he is not also the chief executive officer, has the same communication impedance factors to deal with. Often the chairman has more time and opportunity to seek and accept objective outside counseling. Medium-size and small firms that cannot easily command name directors may therefore seek professional directors.

3. The large investor group, such as a bank, investment fund, or large shareowner, whether or not it has formal representation on the board, often needs a source of professional counsel on the affairs of the enterprise. This is in addition to the information received officially from the chairman and chief executive officer and other captive board members. Closely held corporations may fit this category, where professional counsel is needed without interfering with the family holdings.

4. The top management team often needs access to objective counsel, which can be made available through appropriate use of an outside professional director with the consent of the chief executive officer.

5. The investing public views with interest the presence of an outside professional director on the board, not only as a source of objective counsel to the management but also as one who will keep public interests in mind. Therefore, a professional

director can be a source of confidence in any stock market appraisal of the company and can create favorable public opinion toward the corporation.

6. Meaningful professional nonexecutive director positions can afford (a) an attractive outlook for second-career men, (b) a worthwhile objective of early retirement from executive positions, (c) a clinical opportunity for professionals seeking to expand their horizons, (d) a two-way learning and communication channel for successful leaders in professional, government, foundations, or educational careers who possess the necessary qualifications for professional directorate positions in the business world.

Experienced executives can respond to opportunities to contribute board-level work and counsel in a nonconflicting enterprise in which they are not employed full time. Thus they can broaden their career activity and gain an added sense of achievement by taking on challenging work that is in step with their management experience. Board membership can be intensely interesting and stimulating, can provide new insights and relationships, can enhance prestige, and in many cases can be a way to perform a public service.

Stewardship Duties

The recent public interest in the stewardship behavior of trustees and directors of profit and nonprofit institutions has expanded the examination of the director—his role, his affairs, his practice—from legal, ethical, and social responsibility standpoints. The performance as economic guardian has also been ventilated in the aftermath of such debacles as Penn Central, I.O.S., King Resources, Lockheed, Ampex, Rolls-Royce, Upper Clyde Shipbuilders, Vehicle and Accident Assurance Company (U.K.), and other messy loss situations. *Stigweard*, an eleventh century form of the word *steward*, had different grounds for its early meaning, "keeper of the pigsties."

Only in relatively recent years has the management fraternity devoted much attention to the functions of directors. Conferences, seminars, books, and academic theses, however, are now alive with concern for the director's position, his social and economic role, what is expected of him personally, his liabilities, and the penalties for not performing. There are now institutes for directors, recruiting firms specializing in director head-hunting, and professional groups in the management field specializing in director functions. Unfortunately, there is a paucity of useful information, from a practitioner viewpoint, for the aspirant or new director. To the person who has long aspired to this trustee pinnacle, it is a notable event when he is asked to stand for election as a director—especially the first time. Like a lamb accompanying John the Baptist, the newly elected director often walks into the directorate armed with advice from the friend who proposed him; chances are that he also has some support from his tax accountant, his lawyer, and his wife. Seldom do these advisers and friends tell him (or have the knowledge or courage to tell him) about the institutional theater into which he may be moving. Being asked to stand for a board is something like being rushed for a social fraternity, with all the glamour and symbolism that accompany such secret organizations. Once on the inside, the facts of finances, problem brothers, and demands for continuity and lofty purpose are likely to well up in surprising, if not frightening, terms.

No one thinks to give a new director the lowdown on what it is like to be a director on a specific board, particularly what is *not* expected of him as distinct from what *is* expected. This body of unwritten law that surrounds the director's role is murky and varies over an incredible range of mores and affairs. A guidebook similar to the one given our GIs when they disembark in a strange land should present an overview citing sensitive and cultural points for consideration, as the newly elected director sets out on his career.

On the positive side, the regulatory constraints and personal exposure inherent in directorships tend to overshadow some of the perquisites and psychic returns of being a director. Conflicts of interest, insider information, lawsuits, tax complications, exposure to public indignation, and harassment jeopardize the satisfaction of being a director. There are many benefits to balance these liabilities, however, and they are discussed in the following chapters.

This book is not an exposition on the fiduciary and statutory elements of being a director. Rather, it is a realistic look at the practice of a steward from the standpoint of the director—

steward himself and in the light of the management process and the social, political, and economic processes that are going on at the same time. For example, one of the least recognized phenomena taking place in this scene is the effect on the career and life cycle of individual directors. This is usually out of phase with the trials and triumphs of the institution which is being served. The objectives, style, performance, input, and outtake of a director vary, depending on the phase in his personal career cycle. This personal overlay must be consciously superimposed on the cycles of the institution for which a director is asked to be a steward. "Among all the Talents which are committed to our Stewardship, Time . . . is the most precious."

With all the finger-waving from legal advisers and the public with respect to directors' responsibilities and liability, the recent trend is for institutions to indemnify directors against any activities for which they might be charged in connection with carrying out their function. The armamentarium in this respect is described later.

Director and Directorate Identity

Outside the legal and fiduciary matters, it is well to consider the primary but bifocal problem of identity, which comes into double focus when a person assumes a directorship. This double identity situation in which the director finds himself concerns both the institution and his own sense of himself. A director must maintain his own identity as an individual with an individual sense of responsibility, ethics, and values, and must at the same time serve the corporation. This double identity equation which a knowledgeable director must balance can enhance (or detract from) the institution he serves as well as his own reputation.

The institution may want the director solely because of his status outside the directorship rather than for his personal input. This is sometimes referred to as the *star system*. In some cases an outside director's position and title with his full-time (or former) profession or occupation may be the only real reason for his attractiveness to the board. Acknowledging this identity problem is important because, as time moves on and the director's personal status changes, his welcome on the board may wane. For example, if an outside businessman director moves from one job to another and changes his title, retires, or takes a position in, say, the government or the academic world, his particular value to the original board may change up or down. Realizing that the reason for his invitation to be on the board in the first place was primarily because of his VIP status, a mature director will offer not to stand for reelection.

One person may be invited onto a board because he is a VIP; another may be a distinguished professional or experienced person who is recognized as an individual asset. If an individual is prominent primarily because of his continuing personal accomplishments and wisdom, this factor becomes a problem only if the brightness of the star diminishes—that is, if his professionalism wanes as he gets older. In such circumstances, it should be recognized that has-been stars may not be appropriate candidates for continuing board membership.

Creedal Policies and Practices

The tyro director, who for the first time has been invited to stand for election to the board of a profit or nonprofit institution, should realize the dynamics of the situation in which he is about to become involved. The personal style and influence of the chairman and/or chief executive usually shapes the tone and character of the directorate. This character not only affects

The garage suddenly blossomed...

major policy and determinative matters but often dominates minor activity such as boardroom behavior and dining habits. One chairman has a dislike of cigars so when he enters the board-room there is a ritualistic extinguishing of cigars and examina-tion of the ventilation system. Another chairman has a pet hunt-er's stew he experienced somewhere, which is the routine menu for everyone's lunch regardless of personal preference. Yet another chairman had such a buy-American hangup that none of his inside directors dared own a foreign car. After he died, the officer-direc-tor garage suddenly blossomed with Mercedes-Benzes and BMWs.

Formal board proceedings are only the tip of an ice-berg and perhaps the least important part of boardroom experi-ence from the standpoint of director affairs and practice. The institution will normally see that the director understands the protocol, the litany, and his legal and ethical responsibilities with respect to all statutory activities of the board—no need to com-ment further on that. From the standpoint of the individual, how-ever, there is a need to recognize some of the creedal policies and traditions that seem relatively innocent and passive to a casual observer but are deeply essential to the manifestation of true boardmanship. Subsequent chapters treat the details of some of these traditions and mores.

The subject of compensation always causes both the institution and the individual directors to sit up and take notice. Even the shareowners and· sometimes the public regulatory agencies are now focusing on compensation policies for directors or trustees. Compensation is both direct and indirect, both ma-terial and psychic, and can be related to the dimension of time of career and time of service. The implications of creedal policies and practices in this area are also taken up in another chapter.

Managerial and trustee behavioral patterns follow both rational and not-so-rational styles. The rational process is easily recognized. The nonrational styles consist of a body of knowledge yet to be fashioned into any written or rigid set of practices. There are unwritten axioms or laws which pervade the behavior of the management and of the board. Many have been written as management literature in recent years by Myles Mace, C. Northcote Parkinson, Laurence Peter, Shepherd Mead, and others. A following chapter offers a collection of the tacit "laws" and principles for the tyro director which may serve as directorial rules of thumb.

An alert director will be sensitive to the practices, both straightforward and devious, engaged in by management in order to get approval, support, ratification, and other nods or looks-the-other-way from the board of directors. An adroit chief executive officer is able to lull a board of directors for a long time by the manner in which he conducts his affairs, if the directors are not objective or critical enough or don't know enough about the business to fulfill their check-and-balance function. The dependence of outside directors on management as the sole source of information is a hot subject of debate in some boardrooms. Some of the ploys used by management in getting board approval or disapproval are recited later, as well as the management types to be recognized. This should be of help to the uninitiated director.

Gingering Up the Directors

There was a recent study of the public image of French directors by their fellow countrymen. Surprisingly, the French people hold directors in relatively low esteem; only 17 percent of the replies were favorable, while 70 percent of the respondents were of the opinion that directors were decidedly

An adroit CEO is able to lull a board of directors for a long time.

bad at their jobs. This was so unnerving that a second poll was taken; this one indicated that the public tends to associate the head of a company with fraudulent behavior, wasteful management, and excessive dependence on state aid. Splinter groups from the managerial class have found it fashionable, in France in particular, to investigate such matters and are impatient with the National Confederation of French Industrialists, the *patronat*, which is considered to be too conservative and unwieldy an organization to be capable of introducing much-needed reforms.

The splinter groups attracting the most attention currently in Europe are the Centre des Jeunes Dirigeants (CJD) and Entreprise et Progres. Self-criticism and shock tactics designed to improve industrial relations within the French society are already showing some effect. They indicate that the *patronat* is dominated by large professional federations and has ceased to be progressive. *The Director* baptized the splinter groups as "ginger groups." Allegedly they are in no way politically minded but are intent on a new managerial ideology. CJD had 3,000 members in late 1972, mostly in the 30 to 40 age group, university trained, and majority shareowners in family firms. Entreprise et Progres had a membership of 120 firms, many of them leaders in the industrial field and represented on various committees of the *patronat*. In the earlier years of the Common Market there was a widespread desire for change in French management, and the establishment continues to be attacked. The manifesto is that profits can no longer be a company's only objective; a program of social progress is needed.

So welcome aboard the challenging vessel of the directorship. It is in a period of transition from a Rip van Winkle stage of public consciousness to a space age concern for the world around us. Typical evidence of this is the Chrysler Corporation's recent formation of a committee on public responsibility consisting of three outside and two inside directors. This committee is to examine and review Chrysler's "practices as a corporate citizen to ensure that the corporation exercises leadership in sensing and responding to trends of public concern."

More such board actions are undoubtedly to be expected. The determinative world of the director is an exciting society to be in, and some of the deeper concepts and anatomy of trusteeship are uncovered in the next three chapters. After that come some things to watch out for and be intrigued by, while enjoying the privileges of directors.

3 Honor, Prejudice, and Liability

All persons possessing any portion of power ought to be strongly and awfully impressed with an idea that they act in trust, and that they are to account for their conduct in that trust to the one great Master, Author, and Founder of Society.

Before the turn of the century Lord Justice Selwyn said, "The main duty of a trustee is to commit judicious breaches of trust." In the civilized world one concept of a trustee is a person, real or juristic, who holds property in trust and whose integrity, veracity, justice, and confidence are such that his constituents can proceed on the assumption that his duties will be carried out in their best interests. Trust has been facetiously called what nations have in God but not in each other. Like so many words in our language, *trust* has many meanings; one synonym for it is *monopoly*, implying exclusive control and possession in order to remain faithful to the terms agreed upon in connection with the trust. And it is this paradox which a new director should think most carefully about.

Legally, a director is a member of a committee, called a board of directors, which is responsible for the profitability and continued viability of a company. Corporate directors have been characterized legally at various times as managing partners, mandatories, bailees, trustees, agents, and fiduciaries. Yet none of these terms, if viewed technically, seems correct. Obviously, therefore, the attempt to squeeze the director into one of the existing legal pigeonholes clouds the true picture. As one commentator puts it, the truth is that the status of director and corporation is a distinct legal relationship; further, this relationship cannot be expressed in abstract terms of "trustee" or "agent" but is based on an independent concept of trust and confidence. Accordingly, directors occupy a distinct fiduciary relationship which holds them to a standard of good faith and honesty in all their actions. They are bound to exercise diligence, good faith, fairness, and fidelity and must subordinate their personal interests to those of the corporation.

All sorts of legal, social, and moral penalties hang over a director's head when he accepts this responsibility. Much time is spent in selecting managing directors, chief executives, officers, and top management, but the average board from which a chief executive derives his authority generally just grows, like Topsy. Like Topsy, when a board of directors grows, it marries Turvy, and problems of board composition and membership retirement become most sensitive and difficult. There is limited conscious attempt to design, staff, and operate the board in a manner that is appropriate for the function it is to perform. The honor attendant upon the director position is most critical. Prejudice must not contaminate the exercise of judgment, because the liability of a director is quite extensive. More about these particular standards of behavior follows.

An understanding of the trust carried by a director is important from a legal standpoint. The board as a group and the individual members may come under attack on the ground of personal liability. The accountability of the board of directors to the shareowners is of course shared by all the directors, and each individual director has to take specific action to perform his duties. Even if he does so, and remains accountable, this does not guarantee him immunity from legal action. Such liability is usually concerned with the damages and criminal penalties which would result from an unsuccessful defense against a legal suit. It is these damages and penalties which are of major concern to directors, and it is important that a director have a proper perspective and understanding of his legal posture as a member of a board.

The bibliography contains references with respect to the liabilities and legal framework for a director, and there will be no attempt to duplicate it here. So much has been written about the potential liabilities of directors for errors and omissions or improprieties that the risks are in some cases becoming a bar-

Like Topsy, when a board of directors grows, it marries Turvy.

rier in the recruitment of directors. United States law developed over the last few decades, particularly the federal securities law, has broadened the traditional common-law exposure of corporate directors. The public concern is such that corporate behavior has become a new field for academic, governmental, and legal studies. Typical of these is the analysis by two members of the faculty at the University of Rhode Island, Professors Louis R. Desfosses and Ephraim P. Smith. They have developed a computerized matrix program to study connectiveness among the *Fortune* 500 companies with respect to the composition of their boards of directors. This kind of analysis is seen as a powerful monitoring device which can be used by the appropriate federal agencies to keep surveillance over a large number of companies. Existing legislation designed to protect the investor and some of the loopholes are the subject of the Desfosses–Smith study, as well as suggestions on closing the loopholes and protecting the privileged stockholder.

The extent to which directors and management can be held liable is indicated by the recent suit of three stockholders of a Beverly Hills bank, who sued 24 top officers and directors for more than $350 million in damages, allegedly sustained by the company as a result of their mismanagement. The key to the allegations was that the directors and managers failed to take actions which could have resulted in corporate efficiency and

One of the newer policies is an umbrella liability policy.

savings in interest and penalties. Nor was that all. Allegedly, these people had collected excessive salaries which could have led to the disallowance of unreasonable compensation on the tax return, and they had written off sizable bad debts after alleged feeble efforts to enforce collection. With liability lawsuits on the rise, insurance companies are moving in to review these liability exposures and coverages. One of the newer policies, called an umbrella liability policy, supplements existing coverages by adding $1 million or more for protection.

The duties and obligations of directors in the United States can be classified in two groups: those that conform to the common law and those that come under federal securities laws. Most corporate bylaws indicate that the board of directors has control and management of the business and affairs of the company. The case law generally states that directors of a corporation have the responsibility to establish basic policies of the business and elect officers who will implement those policies. Under common law the director must exercise the authority conferred on him in a conscientious and faithful manner. In considering these duties under common law, focus is generally placed on what are called the duty of diligence and the duty of loyalty.

Duty of Diligence

"Seest thou a man diligent in his business?
He shall stand before kings; he shall not
stand before mean men."

Diligence originally referred to a four-wheeled public stagecoach drawn by four or more horses, which was common in France before the advent of the railroads. It is a derivative of the French word meaning speed and dispatch, as in Shakespeare's "If your diligence be not speedy, I shall be there afore you." A director who is not painstaking, perseveringly attentive, industrious, assiduous, and prudent in carrying out his duties will be subject to personal liability for any losses resulting from failure to perform his duties for the corporation. He is not expected to exercise the wisdom of Solomon, and he need not always be correct in decisions.

A director is said to act in a fiduciary capacity with respect to his corporation, and while he is not typically held to a fiduciary standard as high as that applied to a trustee, a director will be liable if he is clearly guilty of negligence. A fiduciary standard is one founded in trust and based on public confidence for the value or currency of the standard. The moral overtones of standards applied to a trustee are a little different from fiduciary matters and are perhaps best expressed by Anthony Barbour's indelicate question on trust: If you were buying a second-hand car, would you buy it from Harold Wilson?

In some states a director of a financial institution, such as a bank or insurance company, has a higher standard of care applied to him than to those in other institutions or corporations. This higher standard is not clearly defined, but in such matters as investment of company assets there can be considerable common-law type exposure to a director if there are repeated illegal or imprudent investments made.

It is generally considered by various authorities that a director in an effort to exercise the required degree of diligence and care should, among other things, attend meetings regularly, maintain a familiarity with the current financial status of the corporation, give each problem presented to the board his best considered judgment, make suitable inquiry or suggestions as to problems within the scope of the board's concern, register dissent for the record when in disagreement with the action of the majority, maintain an informed position with respect to bylaws relating to the powers and obligations of directors, and adhere to statutory laws which prescribe specific duties to be performed by directors.

In *Litwin* v. *Allen,* Justice Shientag, speaking for the New York Supreme Court, made some significant comments with respect to the fiduciary obligations of a corporate director which, although pertaining to the directors of a commercial bank in this particular case, have been given general applicability to other corporate directors in subsequent case law:

> *A director of a corporation is in the position of a fiduciary. He will not be permitted improperly to profit at the expense of his corporation. Undivided loyalty*

will ever be insisted upon. Personal gain will be denied to a director when it comes because he has taken a position adverse to or in conflict with the best interests of his corporation. The fiduciary relationship imposes a duty to act in accordance with the highest standards which a man of the finest sense of honor might impose upon himself. . . . While there is a lofty moral ideal implicit in this rule, it actually accomplishes a practical beneficent purpose. It recognizes the frailty of human nature; it realizes that where a man's immediate fortunes are concerned he may sometimes be subject to a blindness often intuitive and compulsive. The rule is designed on the one hand to prevent clouded conception of fidelity and a moral indifference that blurs the vision, and on the other hand to stimulate the most luminous critical sense and the finest exercise of judgment uncontaminated by the dross of prejudice, of divided allegiance or of self-interest.

In the subsequent case of *Bayer* v. *Beran,* Justice Shientag had this to say in connection with a derivative stockholders' suit involving a nonbanking corporation:

Directors of a business corporation are not trustees and are not held to strict accountability as such. Nevertheless, their obligations are analogous to those of trustees. Directors are agents; they are fiduciaries. The fiduciary has two paramount obligations: responsibility and loyalty. Those obligations apply with equal force to the humblest agent or broker and to the director of a great and powerful corporation. They lie at the very foundation of our whole system of free private enterprise and are as fresh and significant today as when they were formulated decades ago. . . . The concept of loyalty, of constant, unqualified fidelity, has a definite and precise meaning. The fiduciary must subordinate his individual and private interests to his duty to the corporation whenever the two conflict. . . . A director is not an insurer. On the one hand, he is not called upon to use an extraordinary degree of care and prudence; and on the other hand it is established by the cases that it is not enough for a director to be honest, that fraud is not the orbit of his liability. The director may not act as a dummy or a figurehead. He is called upon to use care, to exercise judgment, the degree of care, the kind of judgment that one would give in similar situations to the conduct of his own affairs. . . .

Duty of Loyalty

Loyalty means more than being true to someone at the top. Because of the fiduciary nature of the situation, a director is held to a high degree of loyalty and fairness in his dealing with the corporation. There are three basic types of cases frequently used to illustrate a corporate director's duty of loyalty to his company:

1. A director is prohibited from taking personal advantage of a business opportunity which in fairness belongs to his corporation. This is the so-called doctrine of corporate opportunity.

2. If a director has an interest in a contract with the firm of which he is a director, he must be prepared to bear the burden of proving the basic good faith involved in the business dealing with the company as well as the equity of the transaction from the viewpoint of the company. For example, it might not be appropriate for a company to enter into an investment transaction with another corporation or unincorporated business if a director holds a beneficial interest of 5 percent or more of such business.

3. A director's duty of loyalty includes the avoidance of direct competition with the company's business activities through another business in which he has a personal interest. This relates to the Clayton Act, Section 8, prohibiting interlocking directorates on the boards of competing companies.

Liability for Breach of Duty

Should a director's duty of diligence or loyalty be breached and result in measurable damage to his corporation, he may be subject to liability for damages in a civil action. If he has breached his duty of diligence, the damages will be in an amount sufficient to compensate the corporation for his negligence. Where a breach of loyalty is found, the director must return any profit on the transaction that is the subject of complaint. Except in certain cases that come under securities laws, directors are generally not exposed to criminal liability. In the event of an alleged breach of duty, a corporate director is most likely to be subject to one of two types of civil actions: a class action or a shareholders' derivative suit, which are subjects for a legal discussion.

The heavy liability of corporate directors leads to a growing legal distinction among three classes of directors, with liabilities defined accordingly:

1. The *single-capacity director,* whose sole significant relationship to the board is in his board membership. This is a typical outside nonexecutive director.

2. The *dual-capacity director,* who either represents a major shareholder bloc and is not a part of management, or is on the board because he is a company executive.

3. The *triple-capacity director,* who is a substantial shareholder or is closely allied with the major shareholder group. In addition to a place on the board, he has a place in the management. This is the case particularly in closely held corporations.

There is a trend in both federal and state legal decisions to impose the highest standards on the triple-capacity director, relax it progressively in favor of a dual-capacity director, and accept from a single-capacity director a performance considerably less arduous, provided there is good faith evident.

The federal reports in recent years have come up with significant decisions in the widely publicized case of *SEC* v. *Texas Gulf Sulphur Company* and in the *Escott* v. *BarChris Construction Company* case, which dealt with disclosure and insider stock transaction matters. In the case of *Escott* v. *BarChris* the liability of directors, accountants, lawyers, and underwriters in the securities prospectus and registration statements was extended considerably. What this ruling warns is that no director can rely solely on the word of management or other experts; he must make a reasonable investigation on his own. The judge held all the defendants liable for the allegedly misleading prospectus, including one director who had been on the board less than a month and had signed only an amended statement.

The Texas Gulf Sulphur decision raised more questions than it answered in the area of corporate disclosure, insider stock transactions, and inside information. The court noted this concern and in its decision called on the Securities and Exchange Commission to use its rule-making power for drawing up guidelines that would provide some predictability of certainty for the business community. Directors and businessmen are becoming increasingly cautious about disclosure and insider stock transactions, even though the court said its ruling applied only to extraordinary events.

Duties of Directors Under Federal Securities Laws

Considered collectively, the federal securities laws incorporate the common-law duties of loyalty and diligence and specifically impose certain requirements and prohibit certain courses of conduct. There are many laws which are of concern, depending on whether the business is manufacturing, financial activities, insurance, or whatever. The legal framework for a particular board of directors or for an individual director will of course be outlined by the legal counsel of the corporation. A director who has any personal concern may do well to ask his own private attorney to advise him also. The areas of fraud—which is a subspecies of absence of good faith—conflict of interest, and negligence are all to be carefully considered.

Indemnification and Insurance

Directors are moving with extreme caution these days, taking out plenty of insurance before they accept membership on a board of directors. According to Harold F. Frederick, president of Stewart Smith Mid-America, Inc., which markets directors' and officers' liability insurance, reported claims under directors' and officers' liability policies increased a staggering 900 percent between 1966 and 1970. As of September 1972, the company had 140 separate claims on file, one of them in excess of $63 million. Executive recruiting firms looking for candidates for directorships understandably find they are hard to finger under these circumstances. Charges against directors include such matters as selling a subsidiary for less than the highest price obtainable; concealing material facts that would have prevented a stockholder from selling his stock at a price considerably below its net worth; firing employees from a financial institution so that a director could secure business from the institution for his own firm; and pirating employees away from a plaintiff's company in order to acquire trade secrets.

Directors of companies are usually protected by an indemnity section in the bylaws and by insurance policies taken out in respect to claims or liabilities incurred or asserted against the directors personally because of actions taken in their capacity as directors of the company, including also protection for the expenses of defense.

Usually, indemnity to a director will be withheld by the company only in three instances: (1) where there has been an adjudication that the director has not acted in good faith; (2) where the director's liability stems from willful malfeasance, bad faith, gross negligence, or reckless disregard of the duties involved in his conduct of office; and (3) where indemnification is prohibited by law, such as in certain securities transactions. Consequently, a director will usually be indemnified totally against loss in any case which does not fall within these exclusions.

A Guide to the Conduct of the Affairs of Directors

Directors go through several stages of concern with respect to their own and the corporate attitude toward legal and social responsibilities. In the first stage the directors stick to the profit and loss statement and balance sheet, products and services, the jobs and growth of the company. In the second stage they make some initial efforts to define the social and environmental problems that are related to their corporate decisions. In the third stage there are full-blown efforts to solve and anticipate some of the problems interfacing with the public, society, consumers, and

A trustee is held to something stricter than the morals of the marketplace.

the government—before they are required by law or regulation or public opinion.

There is a classic wording of this third level of director comprehension and conduct by Justice Cardozo in the case of *Meinhard* v. *Salmon*. While this case involved joint adventurers, the language used has often been quoted as a guide to the conduct of the affairs of any corporate executive, particularly with respect to his fiduciary duties. Justice Cardozo comments as follows:

> *Many forms of conduct permissible in a work-a-day world for those acting at arm's length, are forbidden to those bound by fiduciary ties. A trustee is held to something stricter than the morals of the marketplace. Not honesty alone, but the punctilio of an honor the most sensitive, is then the standard of behavior. As to this there has developed a tradition that is unbending and inveterate. Uncompromising rigidity has been the attitude of courts of equity when petitioned to undermine the rule of undivided loyalty by the "disintegrating erosion" of particular exceptions. . . . Only thus has the level of conduct for fiduciaries been kept at a level higher than that trodden by the crowd.*

4 Director Species

Where Everybody is Somebody, No one is Anybody.

Former *Punch* writer Nigel Balchin, using the pseudonym "Mark Spade, British business authority," produced a delightful book in the fifties on *How to Run a Bassoon Factory,* an intimate guide to business managers and directors. It's still useful. Among other things, he points out that control of a company is not given to the directors; it is vested in them, and he's not sure why. He does proclaim that it is desirable, if possible, to be a director and then itemizes the several sorts of directors: ordinary directors, extraordinary directors, curious and interesting directors, elected directors, selected directors, managing directors, gateleg directors, active directors, sleeping directors, in-directors (avoid these). Mr. Spade says that the functions of directors are important but rather vague. "As their work is almost entirely Thinking, they do not work very long hours, and it is essential that they should spend Saturdays in the open air to recuperate."

A Director Named Charley

In the United Kingdom today magistrates are getting tired of having offenders parade before them who describe themselves as directors, even though legally they are no doubt entitled to do so. A hullabaloo that began back in 1963 was still stirring things up in 1972 over a peddler by the name of Charley Smith, who was a whelk stall proprietor. (A whelk is a spiral-shelled mollusk sold as food in England and often peddled from a small two-wheeled cart, or barrow, in the streets.) Charley bought himself a company off the peg for £25 and thereafter identified himself as a Director of International Whelk Stalls Ltd. rather than a barrow boy. The trouble began when Charley found himself in court for obstruction and described himself as a director, which he was legally permitted to do. Chapter 38 of the U.K. Company Act states, "A director includes any person occupying the position of director by whatever name called."

The irritation of the Old Street Magistrate, E. N. Mc-Elligott—"Today if you own even a whelk stall, you call yourself a director"—triggered a series of editorials and scattered newspaper coverage in 1963. Interest was rekindled in September 1972 when Edward Crowley, a fitter who ran a whelk stall, described himself as a company director and stood £1,000 bail for a friend. Before the court he admitted he didn't have the money and was jailed for six months. When his friend failed to appear at the Old Bailey, Magistrate McElligott said, "You get a man running a whelk stall describing himself as a company director and with all the solemnity that attaches to it, he enters into a recognisance when one knows in one's heart of hearts there isn't ten pence to support it. Nothing in the law prevents anyone, whether he be a whelk stall proprietor or engaged in an even less glamorous profession, from calling himself a company director if he is a director of a limited company." This incident and many more keep up the chatter on differentiating between a genuine and a bogus director. As one observer put it, some people seem to forget that a superior accent is not in itself a passport to respectability.

Like International Whelk Stalls Ltd., directorates in Europe are strongly characterized by the capital ownership feature, perhaps more so than in the United States. Since so much of capital ownership is in private hands, most European directors represent family or closely held capital constituencies. In the United Kingdom, for example, the trend is the same except that financial institutions hold much of ownership, and directors often represent their interests. Too frequently this director role is a relative nullity in the sense of professional determination. Those who are directors in Britain belong to a separate class or "club" of directors which dominates this function. In the United States the composition of the board seems relatively more open to professional director candidates, to inputs by directors from separate disciplines or professions, and to directors with outside interests, that is, a more professional function for the directors.

Legally a director is a member of a committee, called the board of directors, which is responsible for the profitability and continued viability of a company. The directors are agents having a fiduciary relationship to their principal, the company. Not surprisingly, then, there are many distinctly different director types found in the various cultures, institutional jungles, and interlocking directorates around the world. The distinction conferred in most cultures on one bearing the title of director has encouraged the diversification of director types and species. Other than the obvious varietals of junior, senior, male, and female directors, and the relative influence and importance of large as against small, real as against dummy institutions, many other director types are found to flourish currently.

Inside Director or Executive Director

The inside director is an executive, usually an officer and a full-time employee, who also holds a position of director in his firm. Also called executive director, this type of executive or manager has the difficult task of serving two masters, his own top management and the shareowners for whom he is elected a trustee. His situation is almost untenable from a theoretical standpoint because of conflict of interest problems and difficulty in being objective about propositions he submits (or is affected by) when he wears his director's hat. The inside executive director normally is a complete captive of his top management, which determines his career path and survival in the enterprise. In October 1972 David Rockefeller, as chairman of the Chase Manhattan Bank, bluntly announced the resignation of Herbert Patterson, director and president of the bank at a $198,000 salary, thus exposing the plight of captive inside directors. Mr. Rockefeller said, "The outgoing president lacked the temperament and personality to lead the bank in a new, more aggressive competitive phase."

There are inside directors and outside directors.

Outside Director

The outside director is also called a nonexecutive director or a part-time director, since he is not an executive employee of the firm on whose directorate he serves. Further, he usually serves only intermittently on board matters. Outside directors are often representatives of wealthy investors, law firms, or banks, and as directors their judgments are assumed to be less responsive to the management's bias since they normally do not have a dominating vested interest at stake. If they devote time to corporate affairs other than at meetings, they may become *working directors* whose objectivity and ready availability to the management are an important asset. A working director usually receives a retainer rather than a meeting or per diem fee since his schedule will be erratic and unpredictable, depending on his time and the firm's needs. This role has been dubbed "corporate anchorman" or "management's middleman" since the working director, given access to the company's operations and personnel and favored by the CEO, is in a unique position to help weld the board and top management into a more effective relationship. Problems can arise if the working director is not wanted in some quarters, or if he dominates or lacks ability to build rapport.

Lynn A. Brua of Heidrick & Struggles, international executive selection consultants, reported on British and Continental directors as compared to U.S. directors. This was a study of 2,400 large European companies whose directors were invited to

The working director has been dubbed "corporate anchorman."

answer questions about their companies. From European companies 25 percent of directors replied, as compared to 70 percent from the United States. The main focus was the outside directorships held by chief executives. The ranking was as follows:

Germany	Fewest
Great Britain, Netherlands	Fewer than average
Italy	Average
France, Belgium	Many
United States	Most

In Europe, three-quarters of the chief executive officers sit on at least one other board and 32 percent are on three or more. This practice is least prevalent in Germany, where 43 percent serve on none but their own. The French and Belgians are at the other extreme, with an equal share of them serving on at least three other boards. In the United States outside board memberships are even more common than in Europe, with four out of five presidents serving on at least one and 43 percent of the presidents serving on three or more outside boards.

Professional Director
The professional director is also referred to as multiple director. Some especially talented and experienced individuals who have a specialized or generalized capability for dealing with matters likely to be encountered at board level make a career out of serving as director on numerous nonconflicting boards. They institutionalize themselves in this trustee role and are not employees of any one firm, although some may have their own partnership or corporation for tax or other reasons. This director role is clearly one in which the director functions to represent the shareholders. In such representations he uses his individual judgment for the benefit of the shareowners, but he is not a delegate of the shareowners and may not fall in with their wishes and demands. Certainly our system of institutions generally needs more professionalism at the practicing director level.

Statutory Director
In a juristic sense firms are required by statute to have a certain number of directors. Thus all duly elected directors

could be classified as statutory directors. However, there are situations where legal requirements for directors are ritualistically complied with, as in a dummy corporation. Often when firms incorporate subsidiaries or affiliates for tax, legal, or insurance reasons or for public and commercial relations, a number of individuals, junior staff executives for the most part, are named as directors just to fulfill legal requirements although nothing in the way of duties or compensation is expected. Usually officers of the firm or middle management law, treasury, and accounting functionaries are tabbed for this sort of "distinction" because in large firms the number of statutory director spots to be filled on all the subsidiary, associate, and affiliated boards can be formidable. When responsible for international activities of a large firm, I had housemother responsibility for 87 boards of directors throughout the network of affiliated companies.

One well-known property developer in the United Kingdom, Harry Jasper, distinguished himself by holding 400 statutory directorships at the height of his career. Years ago Charles Coster, a partner of J. P. Morgan, held 60 directorships at one time, and Sidney Weinberg of Goldman Sachs, financial underwriters, was once on 34 boards at the same time. This replication calls to mind the definition of a bank as an institution that has a hard time getting all its vice presidents to attend a directors' meeting without giving the public the impression of a run on the bank!

Advisory Director

An advisory board functions as a device to broaden horizons, develop new business, and improve the contacts and trade relations of the corporation, especially in world areas where local know-how is needed. There are few, if any, legal requirements regarding functions of an advisory board or duties of an advisory director.

Living Industries, Inc., a Bronx manufacturer of leisuretime furniture with sales of $3 million, tapped a wide range of outside expertise by creating a seven-man outside nondirector corporate development committee composed of specialists in finance, product development, the sciences, and government relations.

Experience with this group of advisers—the firm avoids the term "advisory director"—confirms that it is not necessary to parcel out directorships in order to secure for operating management "honestly intended, disinterested, and constructive corporate advice at a cost reflecting the real value of the services afforded."

An advisory director is not involved in decision making, whereas the trusteeship role of a statutory director legally requires that he be involved and accountable for certain major decisions affecting the corporation. The advisory director is usually responsible to the chairman or chief executive officer as an individual, whereas the trustee director is responsible to many people, including the shareowners and society as a whole.

An advisory director can perform as an individual counselor to the corporate board, the chairman, or the chief executive officer—and, with proper approval, he can serve as consultant or counselor to others in the company. The advisory director can also serve a corporate situation such as a closely held, sole-ownership or family business, if the time is not appropriate to create an objective, competent outside board of directors. Thus he can provide the chief executive with a resource for testing ideas and actions without being involved in decision making and without complicating the administration of the enterprise or dealing directly with certain vested interests.

Insurance companies, banks, publishing houses, trade associations, government bureaus, and some corporations operating in foreign or regional territory make effective use of advisory

A bank is an institution that has a hard time getting
all its vice presidents to attend a directors' meeting
without giving the impression of a run on the bank!

boards. For example, Chase Manhattan, Chemical Bank, Bechtel, and Controls Company of America (U.S.) employ advisory boards to widen their world perspective. These board members usually have no legal standing, exercise no line authority, and carry none of the responsibilities and liabilities of statutory directors. But they perform their advisory function by alerting the management to changes in the marketplace, in government attitudes, or in public concerns. In return for their services, advisory directors have a chance to meet with the firm's top officers or directors and to gain inside information on the business at hand and plans for the future. They also get to mix with a distinguished collection of other advisory board members on a subject of common interest. Some companies use advisory boards as "farm clubs" for prospective main board candidates. Usually compensation is limited to expenses, some perquisites, and modest honoraria, if any.

Emeritus or Honorary Director

This group usually includes the founder of the firm after retirement, distinguished alumni such as past chairmen and past chief executive officers after their board tenure, and individuals who merit special recognition or opportunity to mix with the board but who are neither eligible nor particularly interested in taking an active part in board affairs. Often large donors to nonprofit institutions are designated honorary directors. Such appointments are valuable when the name and reputation of the individual enhances the board or when courtesy or the political facts of life justify such recognition.

Regional Director

This is an advisory director of sorts whose major input concerns one region or nation because of his residence there. Familiarity with the local scene and reputation make his input particularly valuable to the firm when its base of operations is elsewhere. Usually no legal standing is involved, and the sphere of responsibility is localized or specialized and has only limited representation functions. Coordination of corporate interests, search for new business opportunities, and industry and governmental relations are major functions of regional directors.

Functional Director

The functional director's major contribution is expected to stem from his specialized knowledge, profession, or experience. Bankers, lawyers, educators, clergymen, economists, insurance experts, accountants, and former military or government officials are typical functional directors. Although they are chosen for their special talents or contacts, they are bound to serve in the full capacity as directors when elected. In certain nonprofit institutions an expert fund raiser may be put on the board as recognition of his services or donations. The functional director may also qualify as inside, outside, advisory, or professional director and of course is also a statutory director.

Minority Group Director

With recent social pressures forcing recognition of all sorts of minority groups and "affirmative action" interests, there has been a scramble to respond with a sprinkling of race, color, creed, and sex representatives as directors. The problem here is at least twofold: finding qualified, interested candidates and getting the traditional establishment board to change its thinking sufficiently to go beyond tokenism and welcome responsible seating of a minority group director in the inner board circle. The frequency of such elections is increasing in the more progressive directorates, but the long-term problem will be to find qualified candidates.

The types of directors include emeritus, regional, minority, decorative.

Union or Employee-Group Director

Co-determination laws in Germany (mitbestimmung) and certain other European countries in particular have forced boards to accept employee representatives on the board or council. The consequences of this is a subject in itself, and the trend is spreading. In the United States the Phillips–Van Heusen board of directors recently made a move to give employees a voice in voting proxies of securities held by their pension funds. A committee of young middle managers was selected to do the voting. Their charter: Give concern to good "corporate citizenship" and the "quality of life."

Decision-making conflicts between the wage earners and the owners of capital are sometimes wholly or partly resolved by having elected wage-earning employees serve on supervisory boards or councils. Various similar arrangements are in force in some of the centrally planned economic institutions of Yugoslavia, where major national enterprises deal through Workers' Councils. These models of participation schemes help in softening the impact of certain unpopular measures which have to be taken in the long-term interests of the institution. They also have obvious value in communication and in raising questions about politically sensitive matters such as profit distribution or major personnel problems. (See also Supervisory Director.)

Controlling Director

This is a tax definition for a major shareholder director. The position usually comes into being when the founder, or an early investor, or the major shareowner of an acquired or merged firm holds sufficient stock that a position on the board is warranted or negotiated. In the United Kingdom the Income and Corporation Taxes Act of October 1970 defines a controlling director as one having 5 percent or more of the share capital of a company whose directors jointly have a controlling interest.

Controlling directors can hold a whip hand over the appointment of directors and managers, allocation of capital, and other determinative matters. However, the "doctrine of oppression" used by a particular group of directors to influence dividend distribution, selective purchases, or other practices has been demonstrated—in court cases brought by shareowners fighting such oppression—to be entirely unacceptable practice for a director.

Surrogate Director

This director is a substitute and a delegate for an interested party or constituent, such as a financial institution which has sufficient investment in the firm to command a seat on the board. The appointment can be a legal one, but in reality the functional role is not one of representing these shareowners by using his own judgment. He essentially carries out the wishes of these particular shareowners. An individual major shareowner will arrange for a member of his legal or financial advisers or staff to sit on a directorate in order to keep track of affairs and serve as a conduit in making the major shareowner's views known. A venture capitalist may put a bright young staff man on the board of an entrepreneurial enterprise in which there is a financial interest in order to provide some functional expertise to the board or management and to act as a watchdog for the venture capitalist. "The director is really a watch dog, and the watch dog has no right, without the knowledge of its master, to take sop from a possible wolf."

Multinational Director

With United States business becoming increasingly multinational in scope, a need has developed for overseas resident board members, particularly nationals of the country where the firm has major interests. The reverse need is true for ex-U.S.-based foreign corporations with subsidiary boards and assets in the United States. Despite all the concern about this theory, it is surprising to find so little of this local-nationals-on-the-board policy practiced.

H. F. Tecoz, a professional nonexecutive director in Switzerland, wrote individual letters to the chairmen of 300 industrial corporations and banks in the United States to offer his expertise, if they were interested in having a European non-executive director on their board. His criteria for the firms: public companies exceeding $50 million in sales and banks with more than 400 employees. Mr. Tecoz reports that he received 167 replies. Sixty-one respondents answered as if he were seeking employment; 84 answered that it was not their policy to appoint foreigners on their board or that they had an affiliate in Europe whose board members could fill their needs. Only 22 answered that they were interested in meeting him and negotiating when they visited Europe or when he came to the States.

While such a direct approach may be relatively common in Europe and the United Kingdom, this response is not surprising to anyone familiar with the practice of nominating board members in the States. Our procedure calls to mind Groucho Marx's line that he didn't want to join any club that would have him as a member; chairmen and board members are very cosy about whom they invite to join them. The solicitation is usually from the board to an unsuspecting director prospect; the reverse is not considered good form. As for Great Britain, when a director writes to the Institute of Directors in London saying he wants to join, he is told politely that it is not so much a question of joining as of being elected; each application receives a sponsor, and even then an election is not automatic. Just a few years ago refusals of such applications were running two to three a week.

There are recruiting organizations that will gracefully supply candidate directors, usually for a service fee. Financial, accounting, and consulting institutions also sometimes provide this service for national as well as multinational directors. The more common method is grapevine, cocktail party, other board meetings, and person-to-person calls on a friend-of-a-friend chain of contact.

Public Director

Where the government has a direct interest in a firm, such as a joint venture with a publicly owned firm or a government-created entity, a government official may be appointed to represent the interest on the board. The Panama Canal Company, incorporated as an agency of the United States, has the Secretary of the Army on its board as a delegate of the President of the United States. Overseas Private Investment Corporation (OPIC) has an eleven-man board of directors, six from the private sector and five from the federal government. Federal Deposit Insurance Corporation (FDIC), an independent agency within the executive branch of the government, has a three-man board of directors, one of whom is the Comptroller of the Currency.

Robert Townsend, former chairman of the Avis Rent-a-Car System and author of *Up the Organization,* made the headlines in November 1971 when he proposed that each of the country's 110 biggest corporations be required to allocate $1 million a year for a program designed to protect the public interest in the company's dealings. He further suggested that a special congressional subcommittee be set up to select "public directors" for each of the 110 corporations in the United States that he said have assets in excess of $1 billion. Further, details of salary and staff for these directors were outlined.

Decorative Director

Some companies employ the "star system" for their boards by arranging for the election of a well-known star performer such as a retired government official or military officer or an active or retired chief executive of another firm. An actor director for, say, an entertainment company, a star athlete whose presence on the board implies an endorsement of the product, a distinguished professor whose presence lends esteem to the institution are other forms of the star system. One former movie star has incorporated himself for the purpose of selling his name to directorates with not the slightest pretense of offering anything other than the fading glamour of the movies in the fifties.

These star directors usually number one or two at most; otherwise there is upstaging. Their public relations impact, door-opening ability, name dropping, and cicerone-like services can be a great asset to a board that employs them properly, if it keeps the cosmetic input in perspective and separate from the determinative function of the board. Of course, some directors have a decorative reputation plus specialized talents and value judgments to offer a board, but these are rare birds—often persons embarked on a successful second career.

Shadow Director

Not unlike members of Britain's Shadow Cabinet, there are often one or more individuals who exert major influence on a board without the formal designation of board membership. They are persons whose directions or instructions are not necessarily advice given in a professional capacity. Howard Hughes's peculiar method of operating some of his enterprises is probably the most notable example of such a directorship.

In family-held or family-founded firms there is often a patriarchal (or matriarchal) force behind certain boards which dictates certain decisions or directions. This godfather influence and power can stem from a combination of ownership, tradition, and sheer personal domination over individual board members who may be heirs, deputies, protégés, or long-time close friends. Sicilian-born A. J. Tasca of Control Data Corporation of Minneapolis has, as a sideline, studied the Mafia all his life and suggests that major corporations could improve their performance by studying the inner workings of the management process of the Mafia. Sticking to no more than three or four levels of management, in the seven centuries of its existence this unique institution has avoided the problems of nepotism and favoritism since the boss does not fraternize with his employees—just with other bosses. Shadow directors can and do act as godfathers in some corporations and must be recognized as a real-life phenomenon to be encountered in this world of directorships.

Officer–Director

A fairly recent innovation in the directorate world, this position has been introduced along with the trend toward earlier "retirement" from executive responsibilities for top officers in some U.S. firms. With a focus on the topic of corporate renewal, Texas Instruments has had officers-of-the-board since 1967 when two top executives who were also inside directors moved into these nonoperating officer–director spots to devote only a portion of their time to company affairs. Outside officers-of-the-board were added subsequently. These high-level, capable people have the time to study, to think quietly about, and to comprehend the impact of the rapidly changing internal and external environment and its relationship to Texas Instruments' corporate renewal.

In July 1972, Westinghouse Electric introduced the policy of requiring its top seven executives to retire at age sixty and become officer–directors who are to devote their time to socially important issues that affect the company.

Supervisory Director

It is compulsory in Germany and an option to Dutch and French companies to have a double-decker or two-tier system of boards. One is the executive board, made up of directors actually involved in running the company; the other is the supervisory board, with workers represented. Supervisory board members may also be distinguished national figures whose names and presence add outside status to the supervisory board. There are, of course, some aspects of façade to this system.

Nominations for election to the supervisory board in Germany are submitted jointly by the supervisory board and the board of management. Representation of the employees and the trade unions has been required since 1952, when the industrial partnership law came into effect. In addition to employee and trade union representatives, the supervisory board usually includes representatives from financial institutions, banks, science, public life, and often foreign members who are important to the company's international relations. Often, too, representatives of companies with which the firm has close relationships are elected in order to promote cooperation. Nominations for membership on the supervisory board must be approved by shareholders at the annual general meeting.

The primary function of the supervisory board is to advise the board of management rather than act as a control. The supervisory board helps to decide and shares responsibility in the overall development policy of the firm. The board receives a continuous flow of information from management and acts as a bridge between management and the various branches of industry, education, and political life. The matter of co-determination, introduced in the Ruhr steel industry in 1952, sets forth the composition of the supervisory board as an equal number of representatives of shareholders and of trade unions and employees. In the event of a voting deadlock an additional member of the supervisory board, agreed to by both parties, has to make the final decision. This fundamental change in the economic system involving increased union co-determination is spreading to other industrial sectors in Europe. The issue is a critical one in Common Market discussions.

The supervisory director is not easy to understand for those unfamiliar with this European practice. The following "Letter to a Foreign Business Man" should shed some light.

Dear Foreign Business Man,

I recognize that your time is valuable, but I must say we Germans greatly appreciate the fact that you are always so hospitable and courteous when we come to see you. Why, at times we are even made to feel that we are the top directors of the companies we represent!

Our foreign sales are excellent, in fact we are simply forced to blush when we look at our vast foreign trade surpluses. But I feel the time has come to let you in on a little trick we like playing. Your hospitality often strikes us as being simply too great for men in our positions and the reason, I am afraid to admit, is that you are often being fooled.

You see, when we present our large visiting cards, you sometimes are too impressed by our titles. I'll admit that we Germans rather like titles, especially our wives. You know few things please a woman quite so much here as being called "Frau Direktor," or some such similarly impressive name.

The fact is that our titles rather often tend to exaggerate our importance in the eyes of you foreigners. You see, a man called a "Direktor" may simply be the head of a minor company department and hardly known to the top managers in his firm. I bet you are always mightily impressed when our visiting cards bear the title "Generalbevollmächtigter," which means a person with overall power of attorney for his company's affairs.

I have to admit, however, that while a "Generalbevollmächtigter" is pretty senior, his position is only roughly equivalent to that of a deputy board director's director!

The simple fact of the matter is that we Germans are ourselves increasingly being confused about titles. It's just becoming harder and harder to know just who is the top man in a company these days. Why, who would have thought it possible that such men as Kurt Lotz of Volkswagen, Günter Vogelsang and Jürgen Krackow of Krupp, or Friedrich Krämer of Preussag, could all have been forced to resign from their companies, well before the end of their contracts? All these men were the top managers in their companies and were roughly the equivalent of full managing directors.

In this country the 1937 and 1965 companies laws have established a system in large companies of two-tier boards.

The shareholders elect a supervisory board of directors, known as the Aufsichtsrat, and this body appoints the executive board of directors, known as the Vorstand. The laws are fairly specific about the responsibilities of both boards: confusion really ought not to arise.

The Aufsichtsrat is really composed of part-timers. It meets at most about once every three months and has a limited set of powers.

Its chief job is appointing the Vorstand, and Vorstand members are usually given 5 year contracts. Under the law, a Vorstand member can only be fired if he has done something criminal, acted contrary to a decision taken by a general meeting of shareholders or really acted in a manner harmful to the company.

The Vorstand members are in charge of all day-to-day affairs; they speak for the company and represent it; they are responsible for all company matters and plan the company's future.

Of course, really important major questions have to get the approval of the Aufsichtsrat. Such questions could involve a merger, a really large long-term loan and the setting of a company's dividend.

On the whole, however, the Aufsichtsrat is simply not sufficiently in touch with company affairs to take major decisions without consulting the Vorstand and in general, the Aufsichtsrat approves all the decisions made to it by the Vorstand.

Thus, in this country the chairman of a company's Vorstand is usually taken as the most powerful man in a company. The only time you should be really impressed by a German visiting businessman is when his title indicates that he is on the Vorstand!

The problem is that in the recent past an increasing number of Aufsichtsrat chairmen have become unhappy about giving too much power to Vorstand men. Usually, however, the Aufsichtsrat chairman is not in a position to curtail the powers of a Vorstand chairman.

It is quite a different story, however, when the Aufsichtsrat chairman happens to represent a majority of the issued share capital of a company, or happens to be by far the single biggest shareholder in a company.

The company laws helped poor Paul Hahnemann little when Herbert Quandt decided to sack him. Hahnemann was Vorstand director in charge of BMW sales. But Quandt was the company's Auf-sichtsrat chief and owns more than 65 percent of the BMW shares.

At Krupp the situation was similar in the case of Vogelsang and Krackow. The latter by the way lasted just 60 days as Krupp Vorstand chairman.

Berthold Beitz is chairman of the Krupp Foundation, which holds the Krupp shares, and he is also Krupp Aufsichtsrat chief. For a number of reasons he didn't like the way Vogelsang and Krackow were running things, despite their brilliant records as top managers, so he found some pretext to force their resignations.

Of course the Vorstand members can sue for being fired, but this is a pretty costly course of action and they usually settle for a large payment on having their contracts terminated.

The recent increase in the numbers of Vorstand chiefs to have been fired has added to the confusion over who really are the top men in German companies. The rule, by and large, is that the top man is the Vorstand chief.

However, in those cases where one man or group holds a particularly powerful volume of shares, the Vorstand chief could be little more than the lackey of the Aufsichtsrat chief.

The whole situation is complex and my advice to you is to do a little research into the share distributions in the German company whose "director" you are about to meet. The fact is that nowadays you just are not even safe in assuming that your visitor, with Vorstand chief written on his card, is really all that powerful.

With all this confusion it really does seem rather odd that the Common Market authorities want to introduce two-tier boards throughout Europe. The single board system seems so much simpler.

Well, I'm sorry if in the past we have rather fooled you about our importance. Our little status tricks have been good for sales, you know, so we have no plans to change our system. I'm afraid I dare not sign this letter for fear of demotion to a position which will give me an even more impressive title than the one I presently possess.

Yours sincerely,

? ? ?

Alternate Director

The alternate director is a substitute who, when serv-ing on the board, has all the responsibilities, rewards, and penal-ties of directorships. The practice of appointing alternate directors is more common in private companies where caution is taken to preserve the fine balance of control between various interests or where the regular director has to be absent for extended periods. A director has the responsibility to find his own alternate. Policy and bylaws permitting, it is normal in the United Kingdom for the alternate director to depend on his nominator for remuneration.

The best way to wind up a recital of director species is to return to the purpose of a board of directors. J. M. Juran and J. Keith Louden give three simple answers to "Why a board of directors?":

1 To comply with the law.

2 To help the chief executive officer carry out his responsibilities.

3 To act as trustee for the owners of the business.

We might emphasize a fourth answer which is implicit in the first three:

4 To preserve the institution's relations with the social system and environment which sanction the institution's survival and permit its growth.

In fulfilling these functions various species of directors can contribute. "The law does not permit the stockholders to create a sterilized board of directors" was a judgment handed down in 1918 by J. Collin in *Manson* v. *Curtis*. The value of a board depends upon how many of the 19 director types described earlier are utilized by the shareowners, the institutional investors, the chairman of the board, and the chief executive officer. Undoubtedly, more species of directorships will unfold in the future.

5 The Board and Its Directors

The heart to conceive, the understanding to direct, or the hand to execute.

Much has been written about the optimum mix of age, sex, talents, minority representation, nationality, and political affiliation of persons on a board of directors. Some have suggested that board composition should include an organized loyal opposition, not unlike Parliament, to perform as devil's advocate. Directorates no longer are the preserve of an exclusive band of men who were born with a minute book in their hands and a clear career of trustee or shareowning privileges. Recently there has been a quiet revolution among those holding management and director appointments to a point where philosophical boundaries between management and directors in the private and public sectors have become blurred. For example, a director and president of Ford Motor Company became Secretary of Defense and a director–president of Litton Industries moved into the White House as special assistant to the President. In the United Kingdom the chairman of the National Coal Board was drafted as chairman of the board of Vickers, a former head of the Electricity Council now leads Beechams, and the former chairman of the British Railways Board moved to chairman of the board of Metropolitan Estate and Property Corporation.

For every postulate on optimum composition, one can point to very successful directorates whose member and talent mix is just the opposite of the alleged optimum. One factor often overlooked in board composition is that it must act as a pressure chamber, and therefore an alloy of strengths is most useful. Mounting social and consumer pressures on boards are added to normal business and organizational pressures. The pressures vary widely from nations where public and employee representation on the board is required by law to nations that do not yet recognize these factors in social issues. The spread in Europe of co-determination—the requirement that directorates involve employee representatives—is forcing certain adjustments in the way corporations work and in the delegation of authority to certain committees of the board. The composition of a board should provide a range of attributes which involve heart, understanding, and ability to get the task of the institution done in an effective manner through the directorial talent elected by the shareowners.

Board Composition

Perhaps the greatest disparity is in somewhat shopworn viewpoints on the number of inside executive directors and outside nonexecutive directors there should be on an idealized board. Effective directorates exist over a complete range from all insiders to all outsiders. Actually, judging boards of directors by the inside–outside relationship is all but meaningless. Dr. Stanley C. Vance, professor of business administration at the University of Oregon, has developed an interesting analysis in which four basic board types are suggested, along with any number of mutations, mavericks, and crossbreeds. The four conceptual norms are constitutional boards, consultative boards, collegial boards, and communal boards. Dr. Vance warns that if the first three forms of boards lose their vigor and fail to satisfy society's needs, then a new form, presumably communal, will come forth.

Since a board's primary determinative function has to do with adaptation to change, the need is for directors who have the heart, wisdom, will, and vision and who can deal with change objectively. The state and rate of change in the institution's circumstance may indicate that at different stages of corporate growth or adversity, director input should be heavily weighted with a varying balance of director wisdom and know-how. Sequentially or in combination, a board's circumstances may require entrepreneurial guidance, sophisticated professional stewardship, conventional functional skills such as finance or marketing, caretaker management mentality, socially sensitive direction, political acumen, international knowledge, and/or economic perception. In order to find the right arrangement of director talents it is advisable to have a sufficiently large keyboard of director positions and some turnover of individual directors.

Because of the human self-sealing tendency of a directorate to perpetuate its own kind (whether successful or not), there are often bylaw provisions and other outside pressures to force a more representative and shifting membership. It's too much to expect an unorganized, widely scattered group of shareowners to be very effective in changing the composition and tenure of the directors they elect. Too often, neither the board itself nor the top executive management perceives the need for adjusting the board composition to cope with the needs of the time. It is then the outside nonexecutive directors (if any), the major institutional investors, or, in some recent instances, the professional business press or security analysts who must force the issue of board composition by stock market or public opinion pressures.

The candidate aspiring to a seat on a board of directors should recognize what the real-life situation is and what will be expected and not expected of him during his tenure in office. Although his candidacy is theoretically a matter for the share-owners to decide, in fact it is promoted not by this group of owners or sponsors but by a dominant management or a few members of the board itself, with their various interests and objectives. Thus a successful step onto a board roster is usually accomplished as a tacit trade-off of future collegial support of the incumbent president, chairman, or directors. Personal friendship is hard to keep separate. The nominators have built up collateral with the newcomer to their small society by arranging for his nomination and rather automatic election by the normally benign shareowners. This political situation does not always work to encourage objectivity and professionalism in a directorate. But it is an organizational fact of life which can be either an asset or a liability to an institution and to the individual directors. Nepotism and cronyism are not easy to stamp out when they are well entrenched.

In dummy or shell corporations that are created on paper for legal, tax, public relations, or other reasons, almost any trusted member of the firm or institution can have his name registered as director in compliance with the law, without any real duties. The composition of these brass-plate boards sometimes can be an odd mix of characters. However, the title of director—even of a dummy corporation—can have such status appeal and value on a calling card or passport that an appointment can be made useful and an important goal of some individuals.

In Europe, especially, the title of director is highly valued, but European titles and functions can prove quite baffling to an American. Directors, for instance, are different animals from *directeurs,* and boards come in one- and two-tier sizes. The title of director does not necessarily entail board membership, as in the term managing director or director of research. The equivalent or near equivalent of the American board of directors bears the same name in the United Kingdom; in France it is the *Conseil d'administration;* in Italy it is *Consiglio di amministrazione;* in Spain it is the *Consejo de administración;* in Sweden it is the *Styrelse.* In Holland and Germany, where the two-tier board system exists, *Raad van Commissarissen* and *Aufsichsrat* refer to the respective supervisory boards. The Dutch management board is called *Raad van Bestuur;* the German, *Vorstand.*

Like Britain's "turf accountant" title for a bookie, the title and status of *Herr Direcktor, directeur generale,* and just plain director are an important part of European life. As an extension of this status-consciousness, it is not uncommon for registration numbers on British directors' automobiles to command a surprising price for transfer of ownership, since vehicles are assigned a permanent number. Recently, in the *London Times* the registration number KVB 1 was listed for sale at £250 and JJ 24 could be bought for £500. These prices were for the status symbols attached to the automobiles; the cost of the cars was additional.

The British Institute of Management reported the results of a study of the board composition of 200 medium-size and large companies in the United Kingdom. The typical board had six to fifteen members; 80 percent had nonexecutive directors who made up one-quarter or one-third of the board; the consensus was that the ideal size is eight to twelve directors. The chairman was a full-time executive in 65 percent of the companies; nonexecutive directors were on 24 percent of the boards. Of the full-time chairmen, 40 percent were sole chief executives and 12 percent were joint chiefs. The age range was 51 to 65 years. Of executive directors, three-quarters came from company employee ranks; and the trend is toward a younger age, one-third being under 40 years.

The best board composition is one which has group gestalt, provides for continuity, is professionally determinative, is socially responsible, and meets regularly in a substantive and constructively critical mode. A range of perspective, experience, wisdom, culture, education, age, professions, and constituencies can be provided with careful nomination and election procedures designed to create a stimulating and powerful and objective directorate. The real world of directorship suffers from human frailty and, in too many cases, from an addiction to conformity, resistance to change, and a standardization of member types. This has given the establishment a bad report card in many walks of life, not the least important of which is in the youth generation from which future directors, trustees, regents, and governors must come.

In Greek legend, Procrustes was a robber of Attica who placed all who fell into his hands upon an iron bed. If his victims were longer than the bed, he cut off enough of their legs to make them fit; if shorter, he stretched them until they fit the bed. Theseus slew him by shortening him to fit his own bed.

To reduce men to one standard or one way of thinking or behaving is to place them on a Procrustean bed. This is certainly no model for board composition. What is needed these days is a modern Theseus who can remove those who would try to make all directors fit an institutional Procrustean bed. Moral for threshold directors: Watch what bed you climb into when offered the chance to stand for election.

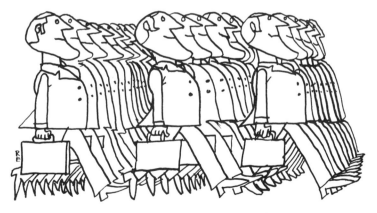

The world of directorship suffers from conformity,
resistance to change, and standardization.

Director Qualifications

Broadly, there are two important parameters providing a framework for director qualifications. The first, which is the easier to qualify under, is concerned with experience and knowledge of directing and managing. Its focus is on the know-how surrounding statutory and regulatory matters, procedures, and the protocol for directorates set forth by government and by institutional bylaws and policy. Management science contributes concepts, techniques, and skills in decision making, planning and evaluation, simulation, and other areas which, if not known, can be learned sufficiently well in sufficient time to satisfy requirements. These areas of intellectual activity are fairly well established and valid more or less universally, with certain national modifications.

The second broad parameter of director qualification concerns the ethical, moral, cultural, and human values perspectives which tend not to be universally accepted or valid. Furthermore, individual institutions or corporations have internal styles, customs, value systems, and cultures that identify with the behavior of the directorate and the individual director's practice. These need to be dealt with separately and should be of concern to those nominating a director as well as to the nominee.

The elements of the first parameter—concerning ordered techniques, hard policy, or law—can be mastered by a

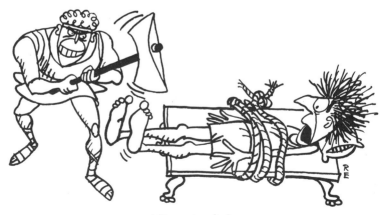

A Procrustean bed.

formal or an informal learning process based on some analytical framework or formal educational setup for imparting such knowledge. The elements of the second parameter—concerning customs, culture, practices, values, and human nature—can be acquired only partly by the educational process and must for the most part be acquired by experience. A knowledge of cause and effect in this dimension is attainable by actual practice.

All this assumes that the prospective director has the basic endowments necessary to aspire to and achieve directorship. Some elements of these two broad parameters of director qualifications can only be mastered in the "director bath of experience." This involves apprenticeship after some conditioning by pre-board-appointment management education and study of the authoritative pronouncements and proscriptions which surround the legal concepts and the statutory qualifications of the director.

To look at the director function in another way, there are at least three strata of know-how important to a paragon director: director know-how, management know-how, and personal know-how. Perfection in all these areas is characteristic only of bachelors' wives and spinsters' children. Anyway, it is useful to consider the desiderata for an impeccable director.

Director Know-How
The ideal candidate for a business firm's board should have a reasonable amount of intellectual capital to offer in four areas:

1. A knowledge of the top management and director functions and practice, plus at least 15 years of successful experience in charge of a key professional, staff, or line function, and/or successful experience as an officer in a publicly owned, profit-oriented corporation.

2. Ability to communicate to others the knowledge and experience gained in prior career activities. A sense of history, intuitive insight, economic instinct, and social sensitivity are among the desirable attributes.

3. Physical and mental capability and vigor, plus eligibility for voting membership on a corporation board, which

by law is accountable to the owners. Such service fulfills the legal trustee role and is distinct from a counseling/advisory role.

4. Intelligent service on some of the many common committees of boards of directors. Such groups may include standing committees or ad hoc committees in the following areas of board concern: stock options, audit, compensation (salary and bonus), finance, executive, nominating, policy, management development, capital appropriations, budget, and investment.

Management Know-How

The ideal director would:

1. Possess a forward-looking, mature philosophy of management; be able to exercise effective leadership of people and/or develop ideas concerning business and management at the interface with the relevant environment of which he or the enterprise is a part.

2. Be able to sense changes, assess public opinion, analyze trends strategically, and evaluate them—when applicable —on an international scale.

3. Be able to identify management problems, evaluate business and economic situations, and consider alternate problem solutions; be a wise judge of people.

4. Have a proven reputation and prestige in top management circles and be able to participate in an interchange of ideas that gives direction to the future business of an enterprise.

5. Possess a reasonable understanding of the skills and tools of some management disciplines (strategic planning, forecasting, organization, motivation, personnel relations, controlling) and other functional skills (marketing, manufacturing, research and development, engineering, finance).

Personal Know-How

Probably the most important attributes of the idealized director concern his personal character. John Cleaver, an American management teacher, has developed a system for assessing personality strengths and weaknesses aimed chiefly at the company boardroom. The self-description test runs through 24 sets of words, such as adventurous, receptive, cordial, moderate, as a first stage in the exercise. The second stage is an analysis in which the executive is fit into the hierarchy. For a would-be director, half a dozen important personal characteristics rate high on the personal quality scale. These are virtues, comprehensions, and beliefs which may be pragmatically stated as follows—and in no particular order of significance.

1. A code of personal ethics consistent with a high level of ethical conduct in the progressive, enlightened world of the business community, including a strong belief in the free enterprise system. Trustworthiness, however, is the key. Unless trust exists between individuals, trusteeship is unachievable regardless of talents and commitment.

2. Recognition that the principal and legitimate objective of the directorate function is to insure that a profit-motivated business renders a valued service to those associated with it as well as to society.

3. A commitment to strive to increase personal competence, keep up with changes, and increase the prestige and dignity of the director function.

4. Use of personal talents, knowledge, and skill in some measure for the advancement of social or public welfare in areas other than his own business enterprise.

5. Possession and maintenance of a high degree of awareness of self-discipline in personal as well as corporate endeavors. Conflicts of interest, insider responsibilities, political and social disciplines, and legitimacy of activities should be constantly in proper ethical and moral focus.

6. Possession of the brain power, zest, personality, and sophistication to cope with the director assignment in a professional manner. This includes willingness to work with, shelve, or disagree with old friends as indicated.

Equipped with a reasonable amount of know-how of the foregoing types, not only should a candidate qualify for directorship but he can probably also keep out of trouble.

It was Voltaire who said, "In this country, it is found necessary now and then to put an admiral to death in order to encourage others." For the person who is eyeing a board appointment and wants to get farther up the waiting line for directorship, the following guides may be useful:

1. A director should clearly understand the difference between being a member of the board and being an executive in the organization and should be able to take a total view at all times.

2. A director should have the courage to express his views in a reasonable manner, even though they are against the majority or against the management.

3. A director must be a logical thinker and a good listener and must be ready to integrate his views with those of the board as often as possible. The time a board member devotes to main areas of responsibility is a matter of good management. At least one-third of the director's time should be spent in monitoring current operations and profit performance, whereas two-thirds of his time should be spent in planning the long-term viability of the business. Unfortunately, the average board usually spends 80 to 90 percent of its time on current operations and details. Examples of proper board matters include:

> Appointment of chief executive officer and top management.
>
> Matters specifically reserved for board decisions by the bylaws or company policy.
>
> Basic policy and organization structure.
>
> Marketing policies, such as whether to enter markets and what channels are to be used or not used.
>
> Significant make-or-buy policies.
>
> Key financial plans and strategy.
>
> Significant pricing policies.
>
> Important procurement plans.
>
> Major personnel policies.

4. In carrying out the duties of a director, certain problems arise which must be dealt with professionally. Here are some of these problems:

> Outside directors often see only the top of the iceberg.
>
> Outside board members do not share a common back-

ground of knowledge and sophistication or interest in the business.

Outside directors can only devote part time.

5. At least three strong forces are complicating the director's task in these dynamic times:

The increased international character of business.

The growing size and complexity of business.

The emergence of new problems which require the board's involvement, such as consumerism and environmental and social responsibility.

In the face of these problems, the information provided board members is usually out of date, excessively figure-oriented, and wholly inadequate.

6. A director should look for certain materials to be supplied him so that he can address major issues and problems of the future. The minimum data would consist of:

Corporate objectives.

Review of the historical results.

Explicit strategic alternate business plans and opportunities.

Examination of financial strategy and forecasts.

Management succession strategy and plans.

7. The information supplied a director should allow him to do these things:

Establish the adequacy, validity, and viability of the company's objectives.

Examine the underlying health of the corporation and its existing business.

Be assured of the legal, audit, and tax situations.

Gain a sound understanding of the present and likely future economic and competitive environment and the problems facing the company in that environment.

Insure that long-term allocation of resources is sound.

Evaluate key executives.

Relate corporate activities to social and environmental responsibilities.

Be assured that the identity and goodwill of the institution are being preserved.

Building a good board of directors requires a good architect who can optimize the board composition so that it functions effectively. The quality of the men and women who make up the board determines its performance, assuming all structural aspects are in good order.

The person who stands for election to a directorate would do well to clarify in his own mind whether the tasks and objectives of the board are explicit, realistic, and challenging; whether the resources envisioned and at hand are sufficient; whether the management talent is available and committed; and whether the organizational structure of the institution is in reasonably good shape.

> *It is not enough to have great qualities, we should also have the management of them.*

6 What a Director Does and Does Not Do

If you have five directorships it is total heaven, like having a permanent hot bath.

What a director does derives from what he knows. His legal responsibilities and obligations are well spelled out for him in most countries' laws and regulations. A director's duties may be collective when acting on a board, or they may be several, or they may be joint and several. In addition to being familiar with the laws of the land and the regulatory framework that may apply, the director's real value lies in his knowledge of the cultural values and ethos of the society; the economic, technological, and political facts of life; and the environmental situation.

There are certain impalpable things that most conscientious directors do in a practical sense. Many activities are obvious and commonplace; others are not so apparent or conventional. An aspirant or incipient director may find the following guides of some help, although each directorate environment is as different as the human beings who make up the group. As in Lord Boothby's bath, the water may be heavenly—or the director may just be in hot water. Common sense is the overriding attribute.

A civil service journal of several years back had something to say about the functions of a director that is worth repeating.

> As nearly everyone knows a director has practically nothing to do except to decide what is to be done; to tell somebody to do it; to listen to reasons why it should not be done; why it should be done by someone else; or why it should be done in a different way; to follow up to see if the thing has been done; to discover that it has not; to enquire why; to listen to excuses from the person who should have done it; to follow up again to see if the thing has been done; only to discover that it has been done incorrectly; to point out how it should have been done; to conclude that as long as it has been done it may as well be left as it is; to wonder if it is not time to get rid of a person who cannot do a thing right; to reflect that he probably has a wife and a large family, and that certainly any successor would be just as bad and maybe worse; to consider how much simpler and better the thing would have been done if one had done it oneself in the first place; to reflect sadly that one could have done it right in twenty minutes, and, as things turned out, one had to spend two days to find out why it has taken three weeks for somebody else to do it wrong.

Undoubtedly this description of a director's job is overdrawn in some respects, but the wonders and worries of directors are by their very nature almost open-ended. From the time of the first boardroom gathering until today there has been little time and relatively little effort spent in clinically studying the area of director practice as distinct from theory and legal constraints. Certainly little has been available at a pragmatic level to help a new director decide how to behave and perform his function.

Any attempt to distill the beliefs and experience of conventional director practice is in itself presumptive. Director practices tend to be less responsive and visible in social, intellectual, and political conflict or control situations than they are in economic conflict or control situations, which are so obviously the purview of the directorate when doing business in the real world.

The directorate system works as well as it does because, down deep, directors themselves believe in certain axioms, whether these beliefs are explicit or implicit. Directors often don't know of or acknowledge that they believe in or behave according to such axioms because in most cases the axioms are so obvious as to need no attention. However, a novice director may not be so experienced or perceptive that these truths about what a director does and does not do are apparent to him.

The following axioms are only a subtle part of the underlying framework of the conventional boardroom style and philosophy of management. In the main it is American-influenced because it is drawn primarily from experience on American boards. The internationalization of boards is a slow-moving phenomenon, but, glacierlike, it is coming. Most of these axioms will probably bear on director habits and mores regardless of national setting.

Perhaps the *first axiom* and the most elementary for a director, novice or experienced, is simply to be prepared. This may sound like Sir Robert Baden-Powell's advice to the Boy Scouts, but we must ask, be prepared for what? The answer covers the full range of individual and group behavior. Trustees are usually individualistic. By virtue of their distinguished position as directors they feel called upon to make significant noises or signals as input to the institution to justify their selection as a major asset. Directors are human beings, and anyone entering the directorate should not forget this in his jousting with the juristics of that legal person, the corporation.

The *second axiom* is for a director to act in a manner resonant with the traditions and objectives of the institution and its executives as well as the mores of the board of directors itself. Iconoclastic behavior which disturbs the equanimity of other directors or the management is bound to cause the same social and political troubles on the board that it would in any other orderly organization.

The behavioral mode of the institution, the executives, and the board is something to be recognized and assessed carefully when one is a fledgling director. The behavioral mode of the board shifts from one state to another as it evolves with time and events. Stafford Beer builds an analogy of the viable firm on a biological cybernetic basis. One of the distillates of his hypothesis is that a firm may exist in many behavioral states, including six modes of sustained activity: growth, retrenchment, crisis, moribund, death wish, and unfeigned aggression. These six states, and perhaps others, can co-exist at periods of time. So it is often a perplexing challenge for a new director to discern just where the directorate coordinates place the firm in these life and behavioral cycles.

The *third axiom* is to recognize at all times the interface between the directorate and the management as well as between the individual directors and individual managers. To mix the determinative role of the director with the executive, administrative, or operating roles of the manager inevitably leads to complications, conflict, loss of objectivity, and misunderstandings. Directors and managers just don't mix well as a rule. The powers that are in the hands of shareowners do not extend to director interference in the management of the company. The director's prime task is to pick the officer management. An intimate mix with the operating management does not usually follow.

The *fourth axiom* is to acknowledge the institution's chain of command at all times. Normally this starts with the chairman of the board as top dog, followed by the chief executive officer; then it links to the operating officers. In each of these positions the incumbent is sensitive to his place in the chain of command. Good form dictates that a director follow this prescribed route when he wants to get information or make contact with the management; otherwise, top management feels its authority undermined. Furthermore, the sense of priority and importance of the inquiry or activity is likely to get out of focus.

The *fifth axiom* is that the sense of identity, gestalt, and purpose in an institution is a most difficult matter which the board has to continually resolve, preserve, or change in order for the institution to remain a viable enterprise. Sadly enough, many firms are *arational* (not irrational) in their purpose. As enterprises grow, ramify, and diversify there must be a strong will in the board to determine future direction and not lose this sense of identity. Identity goes beyond preserving a trade name (Coca-Cola) or an image (IBM) or changing a name (Exxon). All sorts of organizational structural models—appropriations committees, planning committees, acquisition, divestment, and merger committees of the board or management—will evolve in response to the need to reassert coherence and identity in the larger corporations. This sense of identity is a particular problem in conglomerates and in holding companies. A director has a difficult task in pursuing this continual determination of institutional identity in the decisions that come before him in the boardroom.

The *sixth axiom* is that a board's major field of action is in areas of uncertainty, which is a function of variety. Where the risks are measurable, the course is usually clear. Where the risks cannot be measured, it is the board that must use its powers to determine what direction to go in and where to allocate resources sufficient to get there. It is equally vexing to determine whether available resources are sufficient to find out whether it is feasible to go on pursuing the objective. A director who is uncomfortable with uncertainties will have a hard time functioning on an effective board.

The *seventh axiom* has to do with the nature of the board itself, which is an entity of a higher order in organizational systems. The board has certain boundaries, a language structure, and an ethos of its own. The board exists, protects itself in a political sense, and tends to be self-perpetuating; the British refer to this perpetuation as the Old Pals Act. Individual directors are held accountable for their actions and have certain rights and responsibilities; the board as a body is also accountable and has its own rights, obligations, and responsibilities. Collaboration of directors occurs regularly on various issues, and board synergy is an important dynamic of board life.

The *eighth axiom* concerns the internal social life of the board and its members. This varies, of course, from closely knit, personalized board-family behavior to strictly arms-length professional-contact-only interaction. This axiom, albeit obvious, recognizes that the style of social life varies widely with the personal value systems, ethics, and morals of the individual directors. A new director will have to carefully sense the tone of this social and nonsocial life of the board and its individual members and conduct himself accordingly. This axiom spills over sometimes into the behavior expected of a director in political actions, charitable contributions, country club memberships, and even family affairs. For example, one inside director's career was shunted because the chairman of the board considered his marital affairs unseemly.

The *ninth axiom* is that a board will often be more extravagant in committing resources for its own activities than the individual members would be in spending their own time and money. The rationale is usually that nothing is too good for the board members in the way of travel, dining and lodging accommodations, or entertainment when connected with a board function. Collaborative common sense about such expenditures seems to thin out at the board level, as it often does at the top of the management hierarchy. Tax authorities and shareowners' watchdogs are in charge of preventing excesses of self-indulgence, but these constraints are not always effective.

The *tenth axiom* is that the management almost always bestows undue importance upon any director's request. This sometimes leads to a horrendous and useless effort with no thought of justification, merely because a director—usually an outside one—dropped an idle remark or raised a question which was not immediately answerable. Thus a newly elected director should be cautious about expressing himself lest his words be interpreted as a request for an answer to a question that doesn't really need to be answered or cannot be answered without great cost. A director has to act interested at all times, and an exposure to some member of management at a luncheon or on a plant tour often brings on the idle-question syndrome.

The *eleventh axiom* is that in addition to the growth and business cycle of the firm, which is a dynamic the board must deal with, there is likely to be a separate force at work in the board's working practice. This equally potent force is the personal career cycles of the chairman, chief executive officer, and other senior officers of the firm. The significance of these career cycles is usually in inverse proportion to the age of the individual and his nearness to retirement. Career cycle force is therefore relatively short term and never really becomes explicit, because mentioning it would be bad form. A chairman or chief executive officer understandably wants his administration to be notable. It's much easier to launch out in new directions or take bold moves if the consequences are not to be fully realized while you are accountable. Too many times a chairman has been heard to say, only half in jest, "I won't be around when this project comes into its own."

Such a phenomenon is not necessarily irresponsible or inimical to the institution, however, for many major projects have a development time or life cycle longer than the tenure of most executive directors. The derring-do phase comes at a time when the executive has available to him the maximum experience and wisdom he has ever possessed. This career cycle force is one the young novice director should watch for. One example was the chairman who arranged for the golden anniversary of a large institution on its 49th birthday so that he could preside before obligatory retirement forced him out of the chairman's seat.

The *twelfth axiom* states that outside directors are birds of uncommon plumage, but they tend to flock together even though they may represent separate or individual interests. Such a tendency to clique is understandable. The outsiders strive to be constructive and useful, but they rarely have an opportunity to exchange opinions in private, admit ignorance, or investigate their interests and concerns about the management or the firm's activities except in situations dominated by the management's presence.

A good chief executive or chairman is sensitive to any apprehension, perplexity, discomfort, or lack of orientation of outside directors and will exert himself to resolve such spots of disequilibrium on the board. Despite this attention to the care and feeding of directors, there are times when outside directors must communicate with each other, and this is usually done on private occasions unrelated to any board event. Assessment of the chief executive's performance, compensation, and bonuses are official duties normally assigned to outside directors for *in camera* meetings. But there is an irregular, informal, frequent exchange between outside directors, even if only during airplane flights or coffee breaks, or at the hotel suite after the inside directors have gone home overnight before a board meeting. Outside directorships can involve some lonely times. Too bad that chairmen don't better accommodate this need and adroitly provide the occasions in handy places at convenient times. One-on-one relationships between the chairman or chief executive and outside directors are no substitute for the interchange between outside directors.

The *thirteenth axiom* is that directors are traditionally selected according to the crony system despite the myth that they are chosen by the shareowners. This phenomenon, as old as society itself, stems from instincts of self-preservation and the sur-

Birds of uncommon plumage tend to flock together.

vival and comfort of the species. There is a practical and realistic problem in attracting good directors, however, especially from the outside. That problem is the recent focus in the United States on the individual director's liability, both criminal and civil. Potential exposure to adverse criticism from consumerists, environmentalists, minority groups, and all forms of Naderism has made many eligible persons wary of accepting a nomination to a board when they are unfamiliar with the firm, the industry, or particularly the management and directors of the firm. Accordingly, the board's nominating committee, the chief executive, or the chairman (who may be doing the recruiting) is often hard-pressed to come up with likely prospects who have all the desired qualifications and are known to the more influential members of the board. As a result, board nominees tend to be VIP friends, friends of a friend, business acquaintances, or members of service firms serving the board (bankers, lawyers, accountants) who recognize the collateral interests involved in accepting a role of steward from someone who is in a position to trade off such service for some form of loyalty or support at a time in the future.

This is not to say that the boards of directors generally behave like a country club membership committee in selecting new members. But there are elements of this maintenance of a comfortable collegial tone which derives not from snobbishness but from a desire to assemble a collaborative group of persons whose value systems, talents, and life styles are compatible. The trend toward forcing institutions to have employee representatives, minority group members, or public members, plus the awakening interest of financial institutions in having a watchdog representative on the board, tends to thwart the crony system. A newly arrived director can bet his first fee, however, that his known or renowned quality was a factor in his selection for nomination and that the decision was made in a very human frame of reference. In extreme situations the subtle doctrine of oppression can be carried to such an extreme that a director is reduced to a surrogate representative of the chairman, chief executive officer, or other powerful member of the board. The new director must of course sense this situation and cope with it on his own.

The *fourteenth axiom* is that the degree of care and skill a director is expected to exercise naturally changes as standards of expected behavior change and as he acquires knowledge and experience. The responsibilities and liabilities borne by a director are always forbidding, and the reliance he must place on full-time company executives, often colleagues on the board, creates a situation that demands constant study and alertness. Certain legal interpretations have defined the care and skill—in other words, the being in the know—that a director needs to exhibit, and this is generally limited to the skill that may reasonably be expected from a person of his knowledge and experience.

Thus a fledgling director with relatively little experience and knowledge may have a short honeymoon period on the score of being in the know, but his judgments must be prudent, grounded in common sense, and without self-interest from the start. Furthermore, upon election he must become thoroughly familiar with the laws, bylaws, articles of association or incorporation, company charter, and general policies. The nature of being in the know changes, whereas a director's fiduciary trust remains constant by virtue of the position and function of a director, which by definition puts the company's interest before personal interest.

The *fifteenth axiom* dictates certain ethical behavior and a code of conduct with regard to holdings and trading in the shares of a director's company. The elementary rule is enforced by various regulations and laws concerning joint stock companies; it says, do not buy or sell shares (a) on the strength of inside information not available to the general public or (b) without thinking of the possible consequences for the company when you wish to buy or sell. The Texas Gulf Sulphur case is a notable example of the way directors should not behave in such matters. Beyond any personal shareholdings required in qualifying for a director's position, what constitutes a minimum holding is subject to interpretation by the company, the employees, the fellow board members, the chairman, the executives, and the financial community. It is generally considered good form for directors to have enough interest in a company to invest a reasonable amount in it, even though a large holding increases the potential for conflict of interest problems. Other matters of ethical behavior concerning takeover bids, interlocking directorships, and holdings or interests in supplier, creditor, or customer firms are dealt with by the increasing disclosure requirements of the law.

There is nothing magical or prescriptive about the fifteen axioms suggested earlier as guides to director behavior. Rather, they are meant to be descriptive. Directorates do have a touch of mysticism and historicity about them, which beckons to those who do not have access to any such inner sanctum. Anthropologists have discovered past practices which presaged present board behavior. For instance, consider the Council of the Zuñi Indians. The priests of the Council had their sacred objects, their retreats, their dances, their prayers, and their year-long programs, initiated annually by the great winter solstice ceremony. "Since priests are holy men and must never during the prosecution of their duties feel anger, nothing is brought before them about which there will not be unanimous agreement." Similarly, when the Karimojong of East Africa assemble for their succession ritual, "no one must rake up old disputes by asking for the repayment of debts; no one must even beg from another."

My stewardship and trusteeship experiences began appropriately enough in the church, from which modern forms of institutional organizations derived much of their character— along with the management organization concepts of the military. The boards of trustees of nonprofit service organizations can

Nothing is brought before holy men about which
there will not be unanimous agreement.

have more political and social overtones than the boards of profit-oriented economic institutions. These latter have their quantitative framework which dominates the qualitative and subjective parameters of the not-for-profit institutions.

Having been an inside director, outside director, statutory director, honorary director, advisory director, multinational director, and surrogate director at various times on profit-making, not-for-profit, service and manufacturing, trade association, and professional society boards of directors, I have been involved in exciting as well as incredibly dull experiences. At one stage, when I served as coordinating point or major participant in the boards of 87 worldwide subsidiaries and affiliates, the institutions ranged in turnover size from a few thousand to the multibillion dollar class, and the sphere of influence and exposure to vagaries of board behavior was unique. The descriptive axioms listed earlier were derived from these experiences, capped by more recent exposure to some new trustee functions; serving on the boards of five profit-making enterprises and three nonprofit institutions as well as on three advisory boards affords a valuable vantage point for observing trends and changes in style of real-life director practice. Axioms, like laws, change with the times, and new ones are introduced to give some stability to what a director does and does not do.

> We, like the eagles, were born to be free. Yet we are obliged, in order to live at all, to make a cage of laws for ourselves and to stand on the perch.

7 $200 a Day Plus Perks

If you pay in peanuts, you must expect to get monkeys.

There's a hoary story about the man who always entered his pet mongrel in the dog show. He said he didn't expect to win any blue ribbons, but his hound enjoyed associating with such fine dogs. What the man was talking about is psychic reward, which is not unlike one of the most effective forms of director compensation.

There are three general classes of director compensation: real income, psychic income, and perquisites, commonly referred to as perks. Probably one of the best perks is formally recognized in a union contract from which directors are of course excluded: the brewing industry's traditional practice of allowing brewery workers to "tap a line" for periodic beer breaks during their shifts. This may seem to be an insignificant fringe benefit, yet Philip Morris, owner of the Miller Brewing Company, calculates that at its Milwaukee plant alone during two 15-minute breaks a day employees down 2,000 barrels a year! Beer may constitute a perk for employees, but directors are more likely to be plied with champagne and spirits.

Aside from thirst-quenching compensation, it has been said that directors in general are the most underpaid and underutilized people in modern organizations. Surveys by the business press, trade groups, professional associations, and consulting organizations abound on the subject of real income through director fees, retainers, expenses, emoluments, honoraria, and other hard-dollar means of director compensation. (See the bibliography for sources of such information.) Executive directors (insiders) are normally not eligible for this hard-dollar director compensation since their salary and bonus are considered to suffice. The fees ($100 to $500 and higher) commonly paid out for meetings are only part of the income most directors earn. The growing trend is to provide an annual retainer supplemented by per diem fees for meetings attended plus out-of-pocket expenses in getting to and from the meeting place.

The psychic income benefits of directors obviously vary with the prestige of the institution, the stature of the other directors, and the public recognition, values, and popularity of the services or products produced by the corporation. The value of psychic income varies also with the value scales of individual directors. Some are unmoved by the implied power, prestige, and public service recognition that a seat on a particular board provides. Others are motivated mainly by hard-dollar income. Still others, more often than not persons who are economically secure or professionally imbued types, are primarily interested in the psychic rewards of service. The larger tranquilities of freedom, non-involvement in mundane operations, and little responsibility for the plight of the far-off troubled remainder of the system, combined with the stability and status of directorship, are heady psychic benefits to some persons.

One development, "templemania," is worthy of comment since it is often part of a director's psychic income, or is meant to be. Certain companies go overboard on facilities and decor for the boardroom, ranging from a sybaritic suite ambiance to an action central war room setup. These elaborately equipped boardrooms are often part of an overbuilding mania that seems to hit chief executive officers and board chairmen at a certain point in their own careers and the firm's growth cycle. Not all push-button temples for directors are overdone, but many seem to respond to man's inborn desire to build an executive playpen with all the communications paraphernalia and gimmicks that are available in our electronic space age. One inner sanctum has a control panel at the chairman's seat that would vex a 747 pilot. Elaborate security measures are enforced, and all that a numerate

Templemania.

director could ask for in the way of physical and sensual comforts and pleasures are available to ease his heavy thinking sessions.

Perquisites—perks—comprise a more interesting dimension of director compensation. The British and Japanese are particularly adept at devising compensation schemes for employees and officers and for rewarding, by the use of perks, those who hold director seats. In October 1967, the *Asahi Shimbun* ran an extended profile of a typical Japanese "salaryman," Mr. Yano, who "runs on the elite course." While not yet a director, at thirty-six he held the position of assistant branch manager in charge of loans at a well-known Tokyo bank. Living in a three-room, company-owned apartment, he paid monthly rent equal to U.S. $12.50, a token amount in a ridiculously high-rent district. His monthly take-home pay, after taxes, amounted to U.S. $221.40, but this was supplemented by perquisites in the form of meal tickets, commuter tickets, and entertainment expenses. Mr. Yano also gets a substantial bonus twice a year, totaling between 15 and 20 percent of his regular annual salary.

The Japanese have a proverb, *Ebi odoredomo kawa wo idezu* (Though the shrimp may jump about, he will not leave the river), which is particularly applicable to the Japanese salaryman and the director. When they go to work for a company, they expect, and the company expects, that they will be there until retirement. In return for such allegiance, which the Japanese company expects from its employees, officers, and directors, it behaves toward them like a father-protector. The benefits it provides include housing, money loans at low interest rates, most welfare services, free or very inexpensive meals, transportation fees, vacation and outing expenses, and numerous recreational facilities. Ceremonial allowances are given for marriage, for children, and for burial costs of near relatives. If a salaryman is destined to become a director, he is often retained beyond the normal retirement age, which is fifty-five. An interesting perk recently introduced in Tokyo, Nagoya, and Osaka is the creation of a talent bank. This bank is a registry of salarymen and directors who have retired and are available to help smaller enterprises with their experience—a domestic executive service corps of sorts. This not only helps the companies but also provides some second-career income and perquisites.

With international business the way it is, competition forces the companies in most industrialized nations to provide a variety of meaningful perks as incentives for key employees and directors. The greatest draw on perks is undoubtedly possible in privately held institutions and in certain forms of government service, but the perquisite factor in publicly held corporations is an important competitive force to be recognized. For example, how can you compete with Personna's practice in Glasgow, Scotland, where volunteer male personnel have long availed themselves of the opportunity to take their morning shaves on the job, serving as test panels for company products!

Although most company and director guides are mute on this sensitive subject of indirect compensation, the following are some of the more conventional perk forms other than indemnification, expenses of travel, reasonable entertainment, and subsistence when one is engaged in directorate activities.

Charitable contributions. Some companies allow a director or officer to designate the recipient of a corporate charitable contribution. Many firms afford director participation in a matching gift program, with the company matching a director's charitable gift up to a ceiling amount.

Club and association memberships, when a social club, professional club, or association is in any way useful to a director

...where volunteer personnel do their morning shaves on the job.

in connection with his duties as director. Frequently the firm proposes membership (sometimes indirectly through another member to avoid any commercial implications), puts up entrance fees (usually recoverable upon resignation), and pays dues and expenses except when a director uses the facilities for obviously personal affairs. George Washington's "42 basic rules of expense accounting" are still resorted to in this day. His fundamental principle, according to American author Marvin Kitman, was, "be specific on the smaller expenditures and vaguer on the large ones." Describe in some depth the purchase of a ball of twine, but casually throw in the line, "dinner for one army."

Company automobiles with chauffeurs for director activities are considered standard practice in the United States as well as in most countries in Europe, Latin America, and the Far East. One study in 1972 by the Kienbaum Management Consulters, an executive placement and industrial advisory company, revealed that 80 percent of all German company board members rate an official conveyance (plus chauffeur for those in the 100,000 Deutsche-marks-and-above-per-annum category) for business and private use. U.S. practice on this score in industry and government may be less overt than it is elsewhere, but nevertheless it is more frequent than one might expect with the IRS looking over chauffeurs' shoulders. Radio telephones, TV, dictating machines, and bar supplies are not uncommon extras in some director vehicles. Care must be taken not to misuse for personal reasons.

Use of corporate credit for a director's personal benefit is a logical and somewhat conventional practice. Credit cards for communications, travel, hotel and restaurant bills, and so on are frequently issued to directors. The firm's deposit and/or financial credit rating backs up any risk in issuing such credit cards to directors and key employees. In such cases directors can take advantage of the discount rates afforded company employees. Some banks, for example, issue travelers' checks to directors without the usual service fee.

This practice of corporate credit reference is often extended to facilitate directors' personal dealings with banks, law firms, and accounting firms which also serve the corporation.

Such a favored and priority position for bank loans, mortgages, and legal and accounting services is an understandable extension of corporate influence and power which, in some setups, a director may take prudent advantage of as a perquisite of his position.

Director benefit plans. Most employee benefit provisions, such as pensions, group insurance, and hospitalization plans, are not available to outside directors because they are normally considered independent contractors and not employees. Inside directors of course enjoy these benefits, but only in their role as employees. In the United Kingdom some private companies take out life insurance policies on directors' lives and arrange that the proceeds be free of estate taxes while at the same time making it possible for the director to withdraw funds from the company for the benefit of successors and dependents without incurring tax liability.

Special arrangements are sometimes made to provide limited pension benefits for directors of long service. Certain related benefits, such as annual physical examinations, are also provided by some companies. Independent corporate directors who are outside directors and considered self-employed are eligible to deduct and tax-shelter part of their income for retirement purposes by taking advantage of important tax features of the Keogh Act. If a director is engaged in an unincorporated business or profession, he is generally eligible to establish his own retirement plan, deduct on his federal tax return up to 10 percent ($2,500 maximum) of his net income, and invest those funds under a tax shelter.

Entertainment and sporting events are often quite attractive perks. Out of a sense of social responsibility or a need to provide for customer entertainment, most firms are forced to book a company box or a selection of choice seats or tickets to public performances ranging from Yankee Stadium to Covent Garden, LaScala, the Astrodome, Ascot Week, and the Jockey Club. Director priority for such space is usually the highest, transcending clients, customers, and top executive brass of the firm. The British Labour Government of 1964–1970 made a determined effort to restrain what its ministers dubbed "grouse moor living" of directors, and to this end the rules on the tax deductibility of such entertainment were changed.

Christmas can be a most dangerous time of the year for directors and executives. The Yuletide season is held to be a time of goodwill, but it can also be a time for caution because skillful operators often use Christmas parties as the occasion to undermine opposition by politicking and working on the chairman and other susceptible directors.

Executive aircraft privileges can be attractive perks if a director's mission can be connected in any way with the firm's business or if facilitating his schedule can be justified as related to his role as trustee. Somehow or other, wife and family deadheading is often practiced when such aircraft are used for director missions.

Exercise and sauna rooms. The key to the executive washroom is no longer the status symbol it used to be. Recent emphasis on executive and director health has spawned the locker room, private gymnasium, and sauna. With women's liberation a force on the horizon, capital appropriations for these facilities may have to be duplicated.

Loans. Some companies make loans to executives and directors at interest rates lower than bank rates, especially when the loans are for homes, cars, or boats. This practice has some obvious inequities.

Medical attention. Directors usually do not qualify for employee medical insurance plans. But when a physician is needed for a director's ailment, corporate attention goes far beyond courtesy referral to private medical help. It is expected that the firm's professional medical staff will leap with sphygmometer and stethoscope into any situation involving a director while he is going about the company's business. This emergency and interim service is handled according to the medical profession's code of physician referral ethics and jurisdiction. It is a health service to directors that varies from motion sickness and overseas travel pill kits to major consultation on physical problems at the director's request. Far from being an abuse, this personal attention is an understandable perk in this day and age when the care and feeding of directors has developed to a fine art. Annual physical examinations by the company medical staff or the director's own doctor and at company expense are becoming increasingly popular as a perk.

Memorabilia and mementos. Corporate anniversary events, plant site dedications, visits to overseas headquarters, and receptions by subsidiaries when the directorate is on tour often give rise to competition between units of a firm in creating or personalizing decorative or useful articles or displays and in taking group pictures and candid shots that will commemorate the visit. These "totin' privileges" can range all the way from a monogrammed pencil or an attaché case to golf equipment, rugs, articles of clothing, jewelry, books, subscriptions, and foodstuffs. This is not an unusual practice, for the giving of gifts-of-the-realm for visitors to carry away has proceeded unabated since the time of the pharaohs. When not overdone or in bad taste, this perk can be a pleasant one for directors.

Office space and services. Many firms recognize the awkward problem a nonresident director has in running the office required to carry out director duties. Usually the director uses the office and staff of his primary occupation, which amounts to a subsidy. Some alert board chairmen provide office space and secretarial help at headquarters or see to it that directors are reimbursed for expenses incurred elsewhere when the workload justifies it. In the same vein, special parking privileges for directors' personal cars when attending meetings are a common courtesy and privilege arranged by alert board chairmen.

Personal services. Depending on the tradition and style of certain directorates and top management groups, all sorts of personal services somehow can get in the stream of a director's life style. Many perks which are enjoyed by the top management group are also available to directors. These may include executive dining rooms; private office bars and washrooms; contract barber and shoeshine services; messenger and valet services; chauffeurs; private secretarial help; phone, mail, telex, library, and photographic services; and almost unlimited interior decorating service for offices. Personal purchase and investment counseling, tax and legal assistance for personal affairs, personal financial planning services, and real estate and home maintenance assistance are not unknown perks that are made available officially or unofficially, with or without token or full-fee payments.

These practices are, of course, carefully watched by tax and legal experts to avoid misuse, abuse, or adverse publicity.

It is necessary to keep in mind the propriety and justification for any personalized services that are not available to others in the organization and may be considered an improper use of corporate expense and budget allocations. There can be no check and balance if control of such perks is left solely to inside corporate staff who dare not question because they have no clout.

Free (or token payment) access to private suites in hotels at active urban centers, which the company leases for use as living accommodations and as a director sanctum. The Holiday Inn in Gaithersburg, Maryland, has a presidential suite that rents for $1,400 a night. The suite has an executive boardroom, an office that sports a $5,300 desk and a box of vintage cigars, a rococo-modern master bedroom with a working fireplace, and built-in taps that dispense Scotch, bourbon, and martinis. The master bath has a seven-foot-square whirlpool Roman bath that "seats six." Decorated at a cost of $200,000, the six-room-and-bath suite is available for directors, executives, government bigwigs, and diplomats from nearby Washington.

Such expense account elements have been called "arrangements designed to exploit human weakness for the benefit of the firm." Yachts and villas are still provided in some corporate setups and in certain foreign countries. All these arrangements are carefully watched by tax authorities, particularly from a company standpoint.

Retirement privileges. The French have a custom of allowing directors to remain wedded to the board until death or until a voluntary separation is arranged to everyone's satisfaction. One French executive was quoted recently as saying that as long as you stay breathing you can stay on the board. This practice is changing slowly, but it will take some time yet to change tradition. As Sir Walter Puckey, Founder/Chairman of Management Selection (Group) Ltd. and British savant on board matters, has said, "it is easier to let sleeping directors lie." Such retired persons who fill up board seats of course get most if not all the perks of board membership. In countries and companies where the age of board members is limited, some of the retiring sea dogs become honorary or emeritus members or move into other positions of influence or relationships to the board and continue to enjoy some if not all of the perks.

Special travel excursions are not an unusual perk afforded directors, with or without wives, depending on the circumstances and justification. Some firms are more widely known for their parties than for their products. When firms arrange holiday cruises or packaged flight tours as awards for sales contests or for safety recognition, or when they arrange top management visits to plant openings or presentations to security analysts or community events, a director often is invited to take part in the activity at corporate expense. This also educates the director and may stimulate the employees. Since these occasions are usually more social and political than economically characterized, they can be either a source of psychic reward to a director or a real chore, depending upon his interests and his own need for rest and relaxation.

"Test panel" sharing in new products or services introduced by the firm. A new consumer device, publication, fabric, or other product which is of interest in connection with the business—no matter how remotely—may be offered to directors. This is less a scientifically structured panel test than a political and educational practice in director relations which has some obvious values. It takes advantage of the universal human desire to be first with a new product. Conversely—at least in some corporate jet sets and directors' quarters—the introduction of new things is allegedly enhanced if directors appear to sponsor them by the mere fact of possession. Company management jargon for this form of perk is "loot," and its dispensation has to be discreet and proper or the practice can lead to trouble.

Used or depreciated assets. Certain property—office equipment, furniture, automobiles—and lesser items such as stationery and supplies are sometimes made available to directors as perks. The tax authorities usually are sensitive to the market value of any such assets transferred or acquired by directors as a benefit.

James Callaghan, commenting recently on the British scene, probably stated the situation on perks best when he said, "Directors' boardrooms are the top people's National Assistance Board, only they are rather better upholstered." The difficulty here is in maintaining a proper balance between legitimate incentives and rewards for conscientious directors and the abuse of perks. The ethical and moral issues are beyond the scope of this practical guide. Best we should heed the eighteenth century epistle of an English critic of the tastes and standards of his time:

The tempter saw his time; the work he plied;
Stocks and subscriptions poured on every side,
Till all the demon makes his full descent
In one abundant shower of cent. per cent,
Sinks deep within him, and possesses whole,
Then dubs Director, and secures his soul.

8 Funny Things Happen in the Forum

Stafford Beer, Visiting Professor of Cybernetics at Manchester University and Business School, makes an interesting conjecture about the board of directors, which, in his neurocybernetics vocabulary, is called the cerebral cortex or brain of the firm. The mechanisms for control signals in the whole vertebrate kingdom are dependent on certain minute chemical changes which amplify impulses along the nervous system. Scientists have identified how these chemical messengers work in insect societies, and it is a common belief that animals smell fear in human beings. Beer raises the intriguing possibility of chemical messages flowing within a managerial group and suggests that there is a "smell of decision" in a boardroom. However, at this stage of management practice and management science, what goes on in the inner sancta of directorates has yet to have an identifiable olfactory dimension. The twenty-first century director may need to add the smell of decision to his list of things to anticipate as board meeting lore. Note also that Beer's conjectured phenomenon has no connection with the inelegant middle management expression, "That decision stinks!"

The Meeting Is Called to Order
Mark Spade sets forth the general object of a board meeting as rather similar to that of the House of Lords: to prevent any hothead who wants to *do* something from getting on and doing it.

> *A good board, working with proper skill, can usually ensure that absolutely nothing is ever done at all. Even the most hotheaded of managing directors shrinks from the prospect of leading the average board step by step and point by point, through a lot of technicalities, through a constant barrage of keen, shrewd criticism from people who have never heard of the thing he's talking about.*

Because of the very nature of a board of directors, trustees, or regents, its forum activities are ones of inquisition, deliberation, and decisions. The actions are those of a group rather than of individuals. Despite Spade's sarcasm, most boards go about their business with varying degrees of positiveness and decisions toward progress. In such a collective assembly there is of course strength, weakness, tension, conflict, and resistance to change. A board normally operates through a series of happenings called regular or ordinary board meetings and a summary happening referred to—particularly in the United Kingdom—as the annual general meeting or AGM. This signifies the annual occasion when shareowners are privileged to witness and, if they dare, participate in the proceedings. Martin Page refers to the AGM as the one day in the year on which a tribe pays lavish attention to its owners to make up for ignoring them at other times. In simpler times when the base of company ownership was narrow, the owners were the officers, directors, and managers, and meetings were mixtures of board, management, and personal affairs. With increasing size and complexity, the board's determinative function of setting objectives, goals, and directions has had to be separated from the executive and operating functions. The board's accountability to the shareowners and to society should be the major thrust of board meetings.

Regular board meetings are private sessions, usually attended only by official members augmented sporadically by the on-stage appearance of nondirector officers, employees, counsel, auditors, or other guests who have some specific matter requiring their presence at the meeting.

Bylaws of the institution usually set forth the procedure to be followed in announcing and conducting board meetings, in establishing agenda, and in deciding on location, duration, and any protocol features. One critic of the system has defined board meetings as events designed to make company directors feel important. It has also been said that many board meetings are held each month for no better reason than that it has been a month since the last one. However, board meetings are usually serious events. Directors are supposed to do their homework on matters up for discussion. Accordingly, as necessary, documents are sent to members in advance of each meeting. Good management staff work is essential if the board is to perform properly.

Depending on the mix of the board, its balance of outside nonexecutive directors and inside executive directors, and the dominance of the chairman and/or chief executive officer, meetings will vary widely in scope of discussion, questioning, and debate before decisions are made on policy, allocation of resources, or future directions and activities of the institution. Board meetings can vary from a snappy few minutes to those sessions that seem to come to an end only when the directors reach the point of sheer physical exhaustion.

When a board is made up predominantly of inside directors, often its business is decided at management meetings before the formal board meeting. Unfortunately, this can also be the practice with a balanced inside–outside board if the chairman or chief executive officer dominates the outside directors and the board does not function properly as a check and balance. Strategic mistakes can be made when the management staff apparatus functions merely to provide technical justification for a decision already made by top management inside directors. Board decisions made in advance are awkward to reverse at a brief directors' meeting because any outside director with opposing views does not usually have as much background or know-how on a specific proposal as does the proposing management. Thus he is usually at a disadvantage which restrains healthy questioning.

An extreme to which this plight can go was emphasized in the fall of 1972 when Arthur Goldberg, the former Supreme Court associate justice, resigned as a director of Trans World Airlines after unsuccessfully trying to establish an independent committee of outside directors to review the actions and recommendations of management. Mr. Goldberg argued that non-officers on the board should be allowed to meet independently and have the authority to hire a staff of autonomous technical specialists. These advisers would have helped the outside directors to pass judgment on the policies and actions recommended by management. Undoubtedly, the experience of the Penn Central and other cases influenced this point of view that outside directors had a legal and moral obligation to be in a better position to review the actions of management. The other members of the TWA board did not share Mr. Goldberg's view.

The check and balance dynamic of the board–management axis works well in some institutions and hardly at all in others, depending on the situation faced, the independence of the individual directors, the political and social interactions of the directors, and the historical culture of the institution.

The chairman is of course a key figure in conducting board meetings. Sometimes he abdicates this role to the chief executive officer; in many instances the chairman wears two hats. By his parliamentary handling of the agenda the chairman can usually steer the proceedings unless there is overt and tenacious opposition of the type which in recent times has made newspaper headlines over proxy fights, lawsuits, insider and conflict-of-interest matters, consumerism, and social issues that may reach corporation board chambers.

The tyro board member will want to be sensitive to the strategies and tactics surrounding board meeting affairs. Like games people play, here are some of the ways directors meet.

The Rump Board Meeting

This tactic is often used and justified when extra briefing of nonexecutive board members is advisable in advance of the formal meeting. A good chairman will see to it that the outside director's level of information on a particular subject is adequate if not equal to that of the inside directors. In order to accomplish this, a rump session may be called—perhaps the night before—with selected board members present.

The opportunity for faction formation, bias building, and political polarization is an obvious human consequence of rump sessions. The risk in rump sessions is that they could get

The chairman wears two hats.

out of control, be sidetracked from their worthwhile and equitable purpose, and develop into a covert dissident group. Furthermore, an effort must be made to avoid a subsequent rubber-stamp
formal session which inhibits the airing of objective, imaginative,
and controversial aspects at a fully attended board meeting.

Board meeting operation in this regard is like other
organizational dynamics where conflict, tension, and stress are
present and the political process functions.

The Dial-a-Meeting

Like Britain's special telephone services, Dial-a-Menu,
Dial-a-Chuckle, Dial-a-Score, and the recent Dial-a-Cure for advice on the treatment of venereal disease, the telephone is often
used there and in the United States to get directors' advice and
consent and sometimes to "hold" a directors' meeting. In certain
routine or crisis situations the logistics of getting a scattered
quorum of directors together in a hurry can be eased with a conference telephone call or, more likely, a call from the chairman
or president to each director, explaining the action to be taken or
the vote needed. Bylaws permitting, such a meeting is usually
followed up with the necessary confirming paperwork to support
the dial-a-meeting. The Picture-phone and closed circuit TV
are also used for some meetings when geography and time pressures justify. A well-known Manhattan bank with part of its
offices in Wall Street and part in midtown New York regularly
uses closed circuit television for board meetings. It is reported
that the visual effect is so natural that when a lady enters one of
the rooms, the men all rise in both rooms.

The Mobile Meeting

Like floating crap games, some board meetings are
held in strange places: on shipboard, in private aircraft, in hang-
ars, in hotel suites, in manufacturing plants, in fishing and hunting lodges, and in other remote or exotic spots. The floating
meeting vogue has been challenged so often by tax authorities
or public relations advisers that the expense and justification of
meeting in an unconventional locale are always carefully considered.

The advantages to the directors are obvious. There is an opportunity to enjoy a relaxed atmosphere, visit a company property or potential project, give recognition to employee groups or communities, and so on. Besides the need for justifying the extra expense, the disadvantage is the irregularity of such arrangements and facilities plus the logistics of transporting a large number of directors. The separation and distribution of key managers and directors into different aircraft to avoid a corporate tragedy has more protocol problems than a White House dinner party. One company employed three jets and two helicopters for a directors' outing, with more topside, advance, detailed preparation than the project they were inspecting seemed to require.

Considering the assortment of board meeting locations, the candidate director should realize that a director's togs are not limited to Brooks Brothers pinstripes but may include duckblind gear and equipment as well. One junior director found himself investing in new, top-quality golf, hunting, fishing, and arctic gear and garments within two years of his election to the board.

The Statutory Meeting

Although meetings of the board are usually required by statute, the statutory meeting is the often dull and boring but

The mobile meeting is held in strange places.

legally required meeting in which the secretary or clerk of the board dominates the agenda with a variety of required resolutions, approvals, and statements. Like securing a ship at harbor, certain acts must be performed to secure the institution in the environment which sanctions it. Tax, legal, policy, financial, and other votes are usually prewritten in exact form for presentation and ratification at such meetings. The dummy or shell board engages in this kind of meeting as its main organic function.

Depending on the sophistication and personality of the chairman, the secretary, the legal counsel, and other advisers, the statutory meeting can be carried out in somber or breezy fashion. In regulated businesses, such as utilities, banks, insurance companies, and transport organizations, the coded and rule-ridden ambiance in which these activities must operate tends to carry a rather careful style upward to the board for these routine meetings. Operating companies and social organizations are understandably less formal, and the statutory trappings are often less in evidence—unless the chairman particularly enjoys the performance of such meeting drill. One chairman so enjoys the sound of his own voice that rules of order are enunciated and adhered to with sepulchral sounds and with excruciating attention to legal detail.

The Dog-and-Pony-Show Meeting

This type of board meeting is used for several purposes, including education and diversion. The essence of it is the extra stagecraft involved in presenting elaborate charts, slide shows, sample products, educational talks, analyses of the situation in impressive depth, a series of experts who usually pepper their performance with buzzwords, and many other acts involving sight, sound, or touch in demonstrations and displays. The expense of such elaborate meetings sometimes reaches unconscionable size, as no manager feels in a position to challenge the judgment of the director or executive sponsor of such dog-and-pony shows.

Such a meeting is often justified as a background briefing or educational exercise when the board members cannot be expected to be conversant with some complex product, process, or technology or with an unfamiliar country or business environ-

ment. The problem lies in the disproportionate amount of pre-
paratory effort and meeting time that can be spent on such an act
as compared to other issues of board concern which do not lend
themselves to show tactics. Many propositions can be sold to a
board if enough of the inside members and the key nondirector
managers participate in a full-blown selling effort. The very act
of commitment and determination exhibited by the management
in staging the presentation often convinces a director who believes that corporate will is the key to success.

If not overwhelmed by the presentation, the outside
directors are often loath to spike or spite—even if they have the
votes—any proposition that apparently has the momentum and
intense commitment of the management. Such a rejection can be
interpreted as an indication of the board's lack of faith in the
management. Ideally, there should be a cool, unbiased check and
balance on management proposals before a board in ordinary
situations. The dog-and-pony-show tactic can be mighty persuasive, especially to a new or junior director who is feeling his
way in his stewardship. "Good show," however, doesn't necessarily mean good management, good potential, or good judgment.

Regular Board Meetings

Usually held quarterly or monthly, regular board meetings are the ones where a director earns his fee by participating
in a working session whose propose–dispose mechanism and
power play patterns are the main organic functions of the meeting. In a legal sense these are statutory meetings. With a proper
agenda, homework done, and management proposals professionally prepared and not overpresented, the effective working
of the directorate takes place. One survey of United States firms
revealed that 40 percent of the companies checked never hold
special or unscheduled board meetings in addition to their
regularly scheduled meetings.

The conventional meeting is what a candidate director
expects to encounter when he enters the world of directorships.
Most institutions function primarily through such regular meetings, and the effectiveness of their output depends on the ingre-
dients of good management and directorate posture, proper
exercise of determinative powers, and stewardship responsibil-

ities. Regular board meetings are not often the place or time for creative activity, intellectual exchange, humor, social banter, small talk, or political discussions. Decision making in the areas of top management selection, resource allocation, major change in institutional direction, growth, and financial policy matters does not mix well with noneconomic, behavioral, cultural, or subjective phenomena surrounding a board. Hence regular meetings tend to be—and should be—businesslike, orderly, and logical. Philosophy, compassion, and gestalt seldom are on the agenda but have to percolate through the directorate on less formal occasions. Too bad most chairmen don't realize that this informal exchange of ideas, values, and hopes is one of the most treasured inputs that outside directors can provide, if only the setting and time were made available.

AGM: The Annual General Meeting

In addition to regularly scheduled meetings there are times when formal special meetings of the board or shareowners may be required. The big-tent event, however, is the annual shareholders' meeting. This is an occasion when the directorate is on stage and the audience is made up of shareowners, shareowner representatives, auditors, and key nondirector managers who own at least one share of stock and have a genuine interest or feel they must attend for defensive, security, or career reasons. Press representatives often show up at prominent company meetings if there is any chance of good material, and unless they are shareowners, they are dealt with by means of press releases. Admission to the meeting is contingent on shareownership. Elaborate announcements with accompanying proxy statements and detailed agenda votes to be proposed are normal preliminaries to the AGM, along with a formal invitation to attend. Partly in order to humanize the event, some directors' wives like to (or have to) show up in support of their husbands' roles, or they come as prime beneficiaries. It is considered good form in some quarters for executive directors and aspirant directors to position their spouses in reserved stalls where new fashions are in evidence for the occasion.

With legal, financial community, and social pressures on directors mounting, there is little left to chance in the conduct of the meeting. The chairman, president, and other performers really do their homework, and statements are combed by company scriptwriters and lawyers for the state-of-the-corporation remarks. These great truths become bench marks and corporate fingerprints which are studied for years afterward by all sorts of analysts and those interested in competing with, supplying, taxing, regulating, emulating, suing, purchasing goods or services from, seeking donations or contributions from, or obtaining employment or sponsorship from the subject institution.

Locations of annual shareholders' meetings should have some consideration for convenience and informational features; the headquarters office or a major city hotel ballroom is a usual spot. One practice employed by companies that minimize shareowner participation rather than encourage it is to stage the meeting at a remote plant or laboratory in the hope that no troublesome minority will appear.

Large publicly owned corporations, increasingly dependent upon an understanding of their value by the society they serve, make sure that the messages put forth at the shareholders' meeting are in the best public relations form and that the location is sensible and convenient. Meetings are often the occasion for presenting a year's review in visual form, sometimes including movies of products and activities suitably edited. These pictorial presentations are heavily laden with exposures of the key officers and directors when the public relations staff believes this serves inside and outside interests. In earlier days these presentations were likely to be amateurish, but competition for shareownership and the search for ways to make the organization better understood have pumped up the annual meeting shows to a level that is generally quite professional, sometimes even Hollywoodian.

The balance of form and substance is a delicate one for the chairman to decide so that the AGM is in good business taste, yet interesting enough to be informative and keep shareholders happy. The best show, of course, is one that consistently parades superior earnings performance, since most investors can be capricious and disloyal if the primary economic purpose of the institution is not being fulfilled. That is as it should be.

Although not a direct task for the directors as a group, the *annual report* of the institution certainly involves the directorate. This report is usually issued just before the annual meeting of shareholders and signed by the president and chairman of the board. The preparation of this document is as much a headache for the public relations department as is the annual general meeting. The chief executive officer understandably wishes to report to the shareowners the best possible story of the company and its performance in the past year. Reports vary from the terse, dull ones to the more recent *Playboy* centerfold type. Read by investment analysts, accountants, executives, shareowners, competitors, employees, labor unions, and business school professors, the annual report is a vehicle that needs professional attention to balance press agentry with regulatory requirements and good financial, social, and management judgments.

Because these reports are often self-styled, they tend to be stereotyped, self-serving, and quite dull reading. A good put-on by Pepco Litho Inc., a Cedar Rapids, Iowa, firm specializing in the production of annual reports, lampooned the subject in its 1972 Annual Report of The Acme Hot Air Balloon & Wicker Basket Works. The mythical president, T. Lewis Millsap II, commented on finances thus: Though sales declined slightly in 1972 (three balloons sold as compared to four the previous year), net

Annual reports vary from dull to *Playboy* centerfold type.

profits were at an all-time high. This increase was due to a number of factors—reduced sales expenditures, greater plant efficiency, wise investment policies introduced by the board of directors, and the $2.5 million double indemnity life insurance policy which the company held on test pilot Frank "Buzz" Fletcher.

But back to the AGM. The presiding officer begins by identifying and introducing the directors, usually one by one. He then unfolds the good news and the bad news—in reverse order, so that the meeting can end on a note of rising expectations. As a rule, the highlights of the year as given in the annual report are carefully repeated and impressive-sounding, formidably technical staff or line experts are called on, if need be, to explain troublesome points of performance or outlook.

The nomination, election, and investiture of directors used to be a dull and predetermined part of the meeting ritual since most shareowners vote in advance by proxy and are given no choice except the slate proposed by the directors and/or management itself. Now that financial institutions and social and consumer pressure groups are taking an active interest in many public corporations, additional nominees for election to the board are listed with increasing frequency. While it is better form to propose these nominees in advance of the meeting, this is not always the case; and nominations from the floor of the meeting hardly ever crop up except as gestures of protest or publicity.

The procedures for nomination of candidates for directors are being challenged by a variety of stockholders, and organizations have been formed in the United States to focus this concern. One example is the Investor Responsibility Research Center, Inc. (IRRC) in Washington, D.C., which sponsored resolutions submitted to the IBM, Xerox, and Levi Strauss & Company 1973 annual meetings. The language of the resolution presented to all three corporations is identical. It reads as follows:

> Resolved: that the shareholders recommend that the Board of Directors amend the by-laws of the Corporation relating to the nomination and election of Directors, to establish a procedure whereby the Corporation's shareholders may submit nominees for the Board of Directors to be included on the Corporation's proxy statement.

This change, if ever adopted, could bring about dramatic changes in the dynamics of the director selection process. Most shareholders participate in annual meetings by proxy only, and thus shareholders in publicly held corporations rarely are faced with making a choice among alternative candidates for director. The resolution strives to support the principle of "shareholder democracy," which would place all shareholders on an equal footing with management with regard to the privilege of nominating candidates for director.

The tribulations of Thomas G. Wyman, a wealthy investor, illustrate this phenomenon. As reported in *The New York Times*, Mr. Wyman bought 50,000 shares of General Fireproofing in 1968 because he regarded it as a good investment at $15 a share. The 1969–1970 bear market took its toll on the price of this metal office furniture company's shares and Mr. Wyman was able to buy another 50,000 shares at $11 a share. Being concerned about the negative outlook for his investment of more than $1 million, he attempted to get representation on the board to fill an existing vacancy. The overture was turned down for alleged antitrust reasons; Mr. Wyman was on other boards, one of which produced stacking chairs, as did General Fireproofing, although these chairs were a small part of the overall operations at both companies. The quest for representation resulted in a hardening of positions. The company called a special meeting to authorize a

At one AGM this electric moment came...

move from Ohio to Delaware, where cumulative voting could be eliminated from the company charter. Mr. Wyman succeeded in being elected to the board of General Fireproofing in April 1973.

The moment of tenseness that makes the AGM fascinating is the point in the meeting for questions directed at the board or management. The business press and general news publications have reported the drama which unfolds from time to time, especially with the more prominent corporations or notable directors. At one AGM this electric moment came when a previously unidentified shareowner courteously asked to be recognized. He was, and he proceeded to deliver a speech about the troubles the corporation had encountered. As he delved into detail, the tension of the directors and audience mounted. Scribbled notes were poked at the board secretary, and various staff officers surreptitiously scrambled to ascertain who the speaker was, how many shares of stock he held, and anything else that was known about him. When the speaker had built up his rhetorical analysis almost to the bursting point, he capped his speech with a warm panegyric on the board and the management for their admirable handling of the corporate ship in such troubled waters. The board members' blood pressure dropped, and they slumped in their chairs and tried to regain their composure. The chairman rose to the occasion, shed his defensive demeanor, and warmly saluted the shareowner for his perspicacity.

9 The Minuet of Minutes

The person who said that it is well to leave our footprints on the sands of time but wise to be more cautious of our fingerprints undoubtedly was secretary of an early-period board of directors. As a juristic person, the corporation has a duty to record its formal proceedings as indisputable identification of its acts and presence.

From the French word *minute,* a board meeting minute is a rough draft taken down in small writing to be afterward engrossed or written larger. Such engrossing is a drill which should be watched carefully, if one is to be a conscientious director.

This formal chronicle of the inside workings of the directorate is seldom read and less often corrected by anyone other than the secretary of the board, who is unlikely to disturb the bias of his own "engrossings." The corporation legal counsel will of course edit the minutes, because his task is to be cautious of the board's fiduciary fingerprints. The chairman of the board, too, if he is acting responsibly and naturally, will be sure that the minutes contain enough distinguished footprints on the sands of his time in office. At the same time he will avoid fingerprints whose whorls could later upset the legal, financial, and ethical equilibrium of the business or his career. Personally important to the chairman is the aim to have the minutes reflect a distinguished set of footprints characterizing the stride and impact of his leadership while his contemporaries are extant and responsive. Minutes usually remain benign, but they may become malignant if they should ever be exhumed.

Broadly, as to content, minutes should commonly record only the acts and decisions of a board, not its scope of deliberations—and in support of such selectivity it has been said that a board keeps minutes but wastes hours. Enough record should be engrossed, however, to show that the decisions were made by reasonable men using responsible judgment in exercising their determinative powers. The stewardship role of directors as trustees, regents, or elders dictates that proper consideration be given to all constituencies of the organization—parishioners or shareowners, employees and officers, suppliers, creditors, customers or clients, the public, and the government. Too often this balance of constituencies is relatively absent from the minutes of directorate meetings.

The rising concern for social responsibility and consumer rights presages more attention to the reading, writing, and arithmetic of minutes. Many corporations are reviewing their practice of minute writing and the automatic directors' drill—performed as ritualistically as a minuet—in considering the minutes as "having been read and approved" without any genuine examination as to the substance omitted or any real, synthetic, or circumstantial sense of the actual proceedings. The problems are obvious. Some board matters—prospective officer appointments, mergers and acquisitions, compensation, financing plans, plant shutdowns—are so sensitive that they must be kept confidential until the proper time. The expression of a minority view can be a sensitive point in any legal investigation, and individual directors are understandably concerned about their footprints in the matter. Given the possibility that board minutes will be subpoenaed, the recording option of omission or commission of such matters is a delicate one.

Minutes, like children, are supposed to be seen and not heard at any gathering of the elders, but they should be more communicative than they are. More attention to the discipline of the proper recording of minutes can make them a healthy influence rather than a ritualistic minuet.

Minutemanship

The professional practice of minute writing has various purposes:

To faithfully record what actually happened.

To omit or obscure what did happen.

To condition the reader as to what might or might not happen in the future.

To imply certain caveats, assumptions of power, blame, or credit.

To inscribe, for transmission to others, declarations as required by auditors and banks, testimonials such as a salute of esteem to the memory of a departed colleague, or assertions to some governing or judicial body which requires recognition of certain issues or purposes by those holding determinative powers over the entity.

Minutemanship thus embraces three prongs of the communications plug. The first is to record the minimum required by law and regulatory practice. The second is to add to the legal minimum what the chairman of the board, reflecting either his own bias or the consensus of the directorate, wants to say for the record. The third is to add to the legal minimum what the readers of the minutes want to or must hear. This third communications prong is especially related to auditor, tax collector, antitrust, regulatory agency, and public relations matters. In reviewing board minutes, an alert director will perceive the sensitive mix of the three prongs of the communications plug as they connect the directorate's activities with the outside world.

A good hand at writing minutes will be sensitive to this three-part equation of communication when he is recording the proceedings. Some secretaries take additional personal notes on the ebb and flow of meeting proceedings, and these become privileged documents kept by the legal counsel as a reference source. This has some legal risks but does finesse the problem of whether to include or exclude certain discussion matters. The secretary of the board has a duty to record accurately—or, as cynics would have it, inaccurately—the decisions of the directors.

Minutemanship embraces three prongs of the communications plug.

> *And so while the Great Ones repair to their dinner*
> *The Secretary stays growing thinner and thinner,*
> *Racking his brains to record and report*
> *What he thinks they will think that they ought to have*
>   *thought.*

Approvals of Minutes

As the role of director becomes more complex, fraught with personal liabilities, and subject to investigation and criticism, a new level of concern for meeting minutes or other records of director happenings is added to the normal concerns. A director has varying degrees of concern over his political security on the board; evidence of his contribution of wisdom, objectivity, and influence; his personal rapport and interaction with fellow directors; his insider position; potential conflicts of interest; his own and the corporation's external prestige and image. Thus a director who is sensitive to these constraints will carefully read, appraise, and offer corrections to the minutes of meetings he has attended. If he is alert to the nuances of minutemanship he is also sensitive to any early evidence of impending threats to the corporation or perhaps to his own career. He will be alert to the impression the minutes alone give as factual evidence showing where the directorate and the individual directors have been and what they were up to, as seen in retrospect and perhaps from an adversary viewpoint.

In theory, board meetings should be a final forum where conflict, tension, and stress are resolved and where the selection of management, courses of action, and directions for growth as well as the allocation of resources are dealt with in a maelstrom of interacting forces, opinions, and trade-offs. Such meetings insure that the determinations are equitable and serve the various constituencies and purposes of the organization plus the environment which sanctions it. A board meeting itself should be only the culmination of board activity which, in accord with prescribed board responsibility, pervades the entire prudent conduct of the affairs of the institution. Thus the board meeting should be a "supreme court" session at which the disposition of critical issues is based on homework by the board members and adequate information prepared and presented in advance.

So much for theory. In practice, board meetings are likely to be placid—even dull—ceremonials exuding harmony, agreement, and calm. Accordingly, board meeting minutes often have little controversial substance to record. Too bad, for an insight into the complexity of corporate working existence could be fascinating. The functioning of directorates could be revealed as jurisdiction over many matters and the witnessing of challenge, change, compromise, rhetoric, pique, greatness, provincialism, self-service, intrigue, and differing values and ethics. But law, prudence, and protocol usually act as restraints, with the result that most minutes are formal, stuffy, and as stiff as a minuet.

The formality associated with the registration of minutes is typified by the United Kingdom's Companies Act. According to this statute one important duty of a board chairman is to sign the minutes. If minutes are purportedly signed by the chairman of the meeting at which the proceedings were held, or by the chairman of the next succeeding meeting, they are considered evidence of the proceedings. Minutes of general meetings and of directors' meetings are prima facie evidence only. If the articles of incorporation provide that the minutes are to be conclusive of the facts stated thereon, and there is no question of fraud, "no evidence is admissible to displace the record appearing in the minutes." No wonder there is legal supervision and some suppression of the real scenario of board meeting activities.

Species of Minutes

Channing Pollock wrote that two things are as big as the man who possesses them, neither bigger nor smaller; one is a minute and the other is a dollar. Pollock was referring to measurements of time and money, but he could just as well have been measuring directors' activities since their business is often concerned with time and money. Minutes can be grouped into species for interpretation as to (1) their recording of real acts, (2) their implications as to the sense of the determining body's wishes, (3) their sensitivity to contacts with the outside world, (4) the functioning of the corporate anatomy, and (5) the interaction of individual directors or the lack of it. The minutes of directors' meetings can be further identified as species of the following categories.

Pre-meeting minutes. Like premature babies who appear before they are supposed to, these "preemies" are standard practice by board secretaries who are old "minute-hands." When a quorum of directors meets so as to conform to the law, bylaws, or articles of incorporation rather than to address a major issue or wrestle with a disposition of assets or energy, pre-meeting minutes that have been submitted for approval can often get by as a record of the proceedings. The legality of such preemies is open to question.

The trouble with preemies is that they tell little about the health and welfare of the corporation and certainly do not reflect any exchange or inputs of individual directors. For the most part, they serve to maintain the status quo and leave neither informative nor interesting footprints or fingerprints for students of the board process.

No-meeting minutes. These are the recorded minutes of meetings that ostensibly took place but really did not—except in the minds of the participants. In some situations or countries where frequent board meetings are required by law regardless of the intrinsic need for such meetings, it is not uncommon for records of such gatherings to be sent by mail, along with formal proxy statements, before or even after the "meeting." This practice is often used by "brass plate" companies that are formed for tax or statutory rather than operating reasons.

It is not clear just why the law fails to permit a logical and sensible alternative: to record that in the judgment of the board members all their trustee and fiduciary responsibilities are in hand and in proper focus, and spending the time and money for a meeting is therefore not in the best interests of the corporation.

Mini-max minutes. The length of meeting minutes is often in inverse proportion to the actual time spent in the formal proceedings. Hence one would normally be unable to tell from the record whether the board deliberated long and hard before taking action or whether it held a rubber-stamp session. An ambitious board secretary, on the other hand, can find many statutory and other things to say at length, recording minutiae rather than minutes of a meeting in which little of substance was debated or decided. The proper balance of chronicling what actually happened, what the board chairman or secretary would like to have appear as having happened, and what the reader or recipient of the minutes would like to hear can shift the emphasis from minimum to maximum references in the record. Since the philosophy of disclosure rather than supervision is the basis for most laws concerning companies and directors, the judgment used in this mini-max decision on minutes is critical.

Insider or outsider minutes. Since a corporation is sanctioned legally by the society it serves, one would expect that records of board proceedings would have a strong outsider perspective and be subjected to more scrutiny by the public. However, most organizations devote more time to navel-gazing and matters of internal affairs than to the impact of the institution on external affairs and interests. Because minutes are the private account of a board's activities, it is not common practice to publicize them even to the top management of the institution for which the board serves. For security and competitive reasons the recorded deliberations of a board of directors are often understandably sensitive; hence the custom of having them withheld from general knowledge. In reality, only special interests would care to read entire board minutes, for they are characteristically dull reading. Abstracts of specific board actions, such as appropriation approvals or major policy decisions of a determinative nature, are necessarily passed down the organizational ladder of command on a need-to-know basis in order to authorize specific actions, changes, or events. Certain regulatory and legal requirements must also be served by public announcements.

The time may come when minutes of significant directors' meetings will be more accessible to all those who are legitimately concerned. The insider-sensitive portion of the proceedings could be kept separated from proceedings which are of particular interest to outsiders. If we take a lesson from history, the statements of purpose and functions of the Ephesian civilization—chronicled in marble at the site of this Roman city—set a standard that minutes of modern institutions would do well to follow in recording the true sense of their existence.

The importance of meeting minutes is bound to increase as the behavior and value of various institutions become more interrelated with the societies which sanction them. Times and needs change things. The first clocks had no minute hands; the measured minute gained importance with the complexities of society and the pressure on schedules and time. Like Horace Mann's "sixty golden minutes and sixty diamond seconds," time and timing are vital to individual and group activity. Important determinative activities should be set down in the form of meaningful records of the life of an organization. Their review and approval should be more than a minuet of minutes.

10 The Grim Business of Business

Man could direct his ways by plain reason, and support his life by tasteless foods; but God has given us wit, and flavour, and brightness, and laughter, and perfumers, to enliven the days of man's pilgrimage, and to "charm his pained steps over the burning marle."

Days of thorn and thistle for business will test the equanimity
and sense of humor of directors and executives during the socially sensitive seventies, if not forever. The image of grimness in
the business community generally stems from the Protestant
ethic of hard work and dedication to the job combined with the
Victorian emphasis on the worship of success and money. Laughter is rare in the boardroom.

The uptight corporate mien has attracted what Peter
Drucker calls business gadflies who buzz but do not sting with
their best-selling books. But C. Northcote Parkinson, Stephen
Potter, Laurence Peter, Robert Townsend, and the rest never
seem to tackle the main point for directors: the value of detachment and distance from self.

The Value of Detachment

As he struggles to do his best in the competitive business world, the serious, dedicated chief executive officer needs
to be able to detach himself intellectually and emotionally from
fickle Dow Jones averages, consumerism, outside director pressures, corporate politics, conflicts of interest, insider problems,
mergers and acquisitions, and earnings slippage. Such detachment allows him to gain a perspective on the critical issues that
underlie the social, economic, and political realities of every situation. The outside director is normally less uptight but too often
is so remote that he is like the skipper of a sinking pleasure boat
who radioed repeatedly for help. The Coast Guard replied,
"We're on our way. What is your position? Repeat: What is your
position?" "I'm a director of the First National Bank," answered the
yachtsman. "Please hurry." If directors can achieve a reasonable
sense of emotional detachment it will improve their value as
board members. They cannot detach themselves legally from
their fiduciary and trusteeship roles, but they ought to be more
lighthearted about the serious side of being a director.

Detachment also has value because it allows a person
to be unemotional in the face of criticism and above all to laugh
at himself. Laughter is always somewhat humiliating for the person at whom it is directed, but it is really a kind of leveler. Stratification is a great field for humor, and it is an unusual director
who can laugh at the aspects of this in his own position.

The Dither Concept

During World War II the British devised a mechanical system which used a small eccentric, or vibrating, member to keep the whole mechanism in a constant state of minor but rapid vibration. This component was called a dither.

The British use of the dither was recognition that if the parts of a system are constantly in slight motion, the whole device will be alert and immediately responsive to the earliest evidences of forces seeking to change the position of the system. The dither prevented sluggish delay caused by static friction. It was used in fire control systems during World War II and, more recently, in the design of sensitive aircraft instruments.

A sensitivity to humor can be stimulating in its dither effect; and humor, selectively used, can be a most valuable management tool for social control, easing tension in conflict situations, and nurturing a more creative and innovative corporate climate.

The director who has perspective and an accompanying sense of humor can more effectively relieve tensions that might otherwise be beyond his control. This objectivity keeps him relaxed and able to sustain the inner calm so essential for decisive action.

There is an old Latin adage that laughing is more important than living. One hope for the grim-faced business community—driven, electrified, depersonalized, rigidly conventional, often stuffy—is that it will become a little more lighthearted in its seriousness and more serious about being lighthearted. With a sense of humor, society is at equilibrium. Indeed, the degree of civilization can be gauged by the extent to which society can laugh at itself. Corporate society is no different, just a little too somber for its own self.

Where intelligent and dignified "play" is lacking and restrictions and grimness seem to be the order of the day, officers and employees in a business organization are less inclined to work for the good of the company. They go about their duties with minimal involvement and minimal effort; creativity withers; and the company gets the bare minimum for the wages paid its employees.

In a cartoon in the *New Yorker*, a construction boss, complete with horsewhip, stands before an unfinished Egyptian pyramid and says to the slaves dragging the stone blocks, "Stop complaining. It's an honor to be associated with an enterprise of this magnitude!"

In modern, civilized nations, and in the business world, people will no longer accept an unrealistic value system or hidebound hierarchy.

On the other hand, as many studies have shown, leadership that is too informal and too innovative tends to keep personnel at all levels in constant turmoil, putting too high a premium on interpersonal relationships and creating conflicts as a result of the disparity between aspirations and performance. Slim chance of many boardrooms getting this loose. Most directors and practically all chairmen enjoy the grim dignity of their statutory role.

What business leadership needs is a balance between the formal and the informal in management, such that the system will be open to innovation, realistic, and skillful at handling people as well as problems. The boardroom should not be off-limits to a well-timed humorous anecdote or a wry remark on an appropriate subject. The director process can benefit from gentle, subtle humor. But the humor must be applied with care. Heavy-handed or forced humor, or humor that disrupts the sense and flow of the meeting, is worse than no humor at all.

Director Timidity

Despite all its obvious advantages, directors are generally afraid of humor—afraid to use it and afraid to have it used. Using it entails high risk, especially for a tyro director, and is generally inadvisable until a director is well established and respected. The forces of ego, power-seeking, risk, anxiety, and pomposity combine with the huge aspiration–accomplishment gap to discourage the humorous approach. Yet humor is well recognized as a leading edge of social consciousness; political cartoons and caricatures are evidence of this.

Even with the awakening consciousness of directors to their social responsibilities, there seems to be an aversion to recognizing a sense of humor as characteristic of a healthy way of accomplishing goals in the business world. Maybe this is because directors don't know whether, how, or when to let humor be used in a management or trustee situation. Or perhaps they don't understand that humor is stratified, just as directors, officers, and employees are stratified in terms of privileges, responsibilities, and compensation. A comparison of graffiti in plant, office, and executive washrooms would quickly illuminate the differences in brands of humor. The graffiti in the TWA Ambassador editorial offices is a delightful example of letting off steam at headquarters. "Pitney-Bowes licks postage stamps." "Jim Beam drinks root beer." "Xerox never comes up with anything original." You can't think about these without mentally relaxing a bit.

Very little operating-level humor seems funny at the executive or director level, and vice versa. Too few businessmen, and hardly any directors, have the ability to laugh at themselves. Even more serious is the general atrophy of humor in the boardroom.

It sometimes seems as if the very wellsprings of humor have dried up. Derision is taken for disloyalty; political satire is almost extinct; personal caricatures can be considered libelous; parody is illegal; dialect jokes are strictly taboo; management and labor are sacrosanct; and Huckleberry Finn has been cited as an invitation to juvenile delinquency!

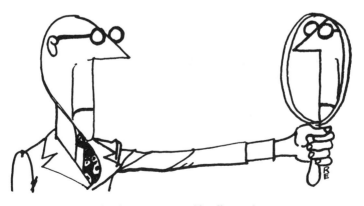

Too few businessmen, and hardly any directors,
have the ability to laugh at themselves.

The Value of Humor

There seems to be no objective evidence that a good director or chairman has a better sense of humor than a poor one, but a pertinent experiment was conducted with reference to teachers. A group of students were asked to rate their teachers according to teaching ability and amount of humor in the classroom (how often the class laughed and how often an instructor told humorous stories). In a study involving 284 teachers, the best teachers averaged 3.95 on a humor scale of 5; the poorest averaged 2.36. Thus a sense of humor certainly appeared to be a trait of a good teacher more often than of a poor teacher. Inasmuch as directors project an image of a teacher by their example or by their style, a sense of humor is an important quality for effective leadership.

If chairmen of boards realized that they could save money by a proper application of humor, they would use it more. Much money is spent in trying to keep directors happy by raising fees, providing perks, and offering elaborate company entertainment. How much it would be appreciated, and how rewarding to the individual directors as well as the board as a whole, if an equal amount of effort and ingenuity were directed toward relaxing the boardroom and informal meeting climate by a healthy, judicious safety valve of humor, displayed on appropriate occasion by the chairman or chief executive officer.

Seals of Approval

It can truly be said that the light touch is medically and historically approved. Humor and diversion have long been recommended by physicians as a means of relaxation for men at the top. And this need and approval probably explains the prevalence of court jesters in the Middle Ages. Furthermore, it's worthy of note that educated masters preferred intelligent jesters, men who could *play* the fool—not simple-minded men. For instance, Cardinal Richelieu's jester, the Abbe des Boisrobert, was a keen wit, scandalmonger, play author, and patron of the arts. Wiegand von Theban, court jester to Duke Otto of Hapsburg in the fourteenth century, was a parish priest as well and evidently was successful in both roles.

A British author, Lord Dunsany, proposed in the early

1950s that a Minister of Mirth and Mockery be established in England on the thesis that "a world of dangerously inflated egos needs the deflating touch of the court fool of old."

Enid Welsford, British author and lecturer, has made an interesting study of the jester. In her view, there have always been men who have a faculty for taking life in stride and gliding out of awkward situations which would baffle more serious-minded and responsibility-bearing individuals. Such characters are sources of entertainment to their fellows. Their company is welcomed. Good stories accumulate about them—especially if they seem to have little conscience and no shame. And they often manage to make a handsome profit out of their supposed irresponsibility.

Today's boardrooms could use a new type of jester—maybe only in shadow form, but one who would serve many purposes in special ways. He should fit in an institution that is filled with a sense of its own momentum and importance and has become a structured hierarchy, monarchical in the sense that it has a strong leader who gives the final go-ahead after reviewing a sophisticated drill of planning, evaluating, and strategizing. The "monarch chairman" sets the tone of solemnity, conformity, and control—or of spirited and imaginative innovation.

If history is a good guide, a modern boardroom jester—adviser could make a worthwhile contribution, even if he simply

Today's boardrooms could use a new type of jester.

helped the board members achieve the detachment that gives them perspective. But the jester–adviser could also serve as a devil's advocate in residence, helping other directors to be a little more lighthearted about their serious, sometimes grim, business and allowing constructive criticism to flourish.

The Sense of Humor in Corporate Matters

Recognizing that a sense of humor is one of the most desirable personal qualities, the board chairman might well acknowledge the importance and place of humor and its value of detachment in his conduct of certain boardroom affairs. Humor, wisely used, can be a potent input to several areas of concern to the directorate, among them the following:

Social stratification and status. In a cartoon, a man and wife are shown reading their evening paper. The wife looks up and asks, "Are we capital or labor?" In another a middle-aged director, sitting comfortably in an airliner, says to his wife, "You fail me in so many small ways, Grace, like reading a paperback when we are traveling first class."

These cartoons strike at the heart of the social stratification issue, which is a principal target of anthologies of jokes and is an inherent conflict source in most business organizations. Status, income, and occupations of the extremes of the hierarchy

Carnivorous aggression—the public's view of the conglomerate.

—top and bottom, rich and poor—are the subject of a kind of humorous leveling process consistent with American values.

Corporate public relations. The public image of business could use some humor in order to test its values and to project its true significance to society. Harvard Professor Emeritus Myles Mace has defined a *conglomerate* as a twelve-letter word with a four-letter meaning, and thus in a wry way has put a finger on a most acute corporate problem. Carnivorous aggression characterizes the public's view of the conglomerate. A sense of humor might do much to take the edge off this biting appraisal. Humor can also help to humanize business by serving as an antidote for pomposity. But it should be recognized that while humor has been found to be a satisfactory means of creating awareness and recognition of an organization or product, it does not convince or persuade in a marketing sense. Therefore, corporate use of humor had best be confined to undermining pomposity and to imparting a sense that the company (and the board of directors) is realistic about its place in the scheme of things.

Avoidance of surprise. Business thrives on risk-taking, but it likes to anticipate and prepare for the risks. Surprise may be far from desirable in strategic planning, but in leadership style it can be used to relax tensions. There's a surprise element in wit that can be useful. This is the surprise of having the expected not happen, rather than having the unexpected happen.

An event can be humorous when the usual result does not occur, as in this updated version of the story of the traveling salesman: A proper businessman, traveling in the British Midlands late one night, stopped at a hotel that was filled. Taking pity on him the room clerk said he could accommodate the businessman, but only if he was willing to share a double bed with a blond singer. The guest drew himself up to his full height and said, "Sir, I'll have you know I'm a gentleman," whereupon the clerk responded, "So is the singer!"

Acquiring political perspective. When we can see our own grotesqueries and droll ambitions, we become less egocentric. So it is with a governing body, whether in the boardroom or in politics. For a director gauging the executive staff, this is particularly true in acknowledging the gap between managers' aspirations and their accomplishments. Boardroom politics is not renowned for its sense of perspective.

As elsewhere in life, humor can be an asset in corporate politics; but a sense of humor may be something else again. The ho-ho-ho kind of humor emanates from the man who lives on the outer layer of consciousness; a sense of humor characterizes the man who lives more deeply within himself. The introspective intellectual is generally considered suspect by those who prefer humor that is more earthy than worldly. Thus wit, as opposed to jollity, is rarely encouraged by advisers to major political candidates. Indeed, many political experts believe that the sharp wit of Adlai Stevenson contributed to his downfall. Boardroom ambiance is usually such that wit is more in order than jollity since it is more intellectual.

Safety and Survival

It has been said that the most valuable sense of humor is the kind that enables a person to see instantly what isn't safe to laugh at. This is important in the conflicts inherent in director and management activities, particularly in the somber sanctum of the boardroom.

In judging the management, directors will readily recognize the situation typified by the blast of one president to his vice presidents: "You fellows better start practicing human rela-

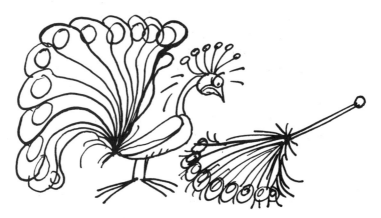

Today a peacock, tomorrow a feather duster!

tions around here, or I'll fire the whole damn bunch of you!" Or the often-quoted plea of the Hollywood producer to his directors, "I want you to tell me the truth, even if it means losing your job." These bits of humor spotlight the survival-of-the-fittest syndrome in certain management hierarchies. Today a peacock, tomorrow a feather duster!

The Punch Line

Like the chairman–monarch, the chief executive officer is considered almost infallible. But a monarch can and does err; the top executive never really has the right to do so. The board has the job of removing him if he slips too often.

Perhaps the greatest function a boardroom jester–adviser might perform, then, if one could create such a position, would be to assume the foibles of his "master" and his cabinet and, by making errors slightly ludicrous, make them more forgivable—perhaps even acceptable. But even here, directors can do a great deal to help themselves, simply by learning not to take themselves so seriously.

As an antidote to the pressures of conflict and the rigors of survival in the executive jungle, humor needs to be better recognized in the boardroom. This is not a new idea. Albert Rapp relates a story of Amasis, fifth Pharaoh of the 26th Egyptian dynasty (about 570 to 526 B.C.). Amasis rose from the ranks and appears to have been a capable and judicious sovereign, living at the time of Croesus and the rise of Greek art, philosophy, literature, and science. Despite this serious milieu, Amasis had a notorious routine. Every day he would rise before dawn and work like a Trojan until noonday. From then on, there would be nothing but merriment. The barley brew flowed freely, and Amasis gathered a crowd around him and swapped funny stories.

Historians relate that some of the good Pharaoh's stories were "not seemly." According to Herodotus, one day some of his closest advisers took him aside and told him that people were saying the Pharaoh should sit upon his royal throne and be a symbol of dignity and not a humorist in the throne room. Amasis is said to have replied, "When an archer goes into battle, he strings his bow until it is taut. When the shooting is over, he unstrings it again. If he didn't unstring it, it would lose its snap and would be no good to him when he needed it."

Humor has been said to be the most philosophic of all emotions. Directors are constantly faced with problems that demand the best solution; and being only mortal, they do not always arrive at the right one. Two important qualities for successful directorship are emotional control and tact. The value of a sense of humor and a sense of detachment in gaining emotional control cannot be overemphasized.

In the boardroom of tomorrow, it may be that only he who laughs best will last.

Maybe he who laughs best will last.

11 Unwritten Laws

There is a written law and an unwritten law. Written law is that under which we live in different cities, but that which has arisen from custom is called unwritten law.

The unwritten laws that pervade the boardroom are interesting propositions that typify the constantly changing code of boardroom behavior. These boardroom goings-on can be metamorphosed into laws of nature of a sort. This chapter is a first collection of these propositions from many sources, some anonymous and some identified.

Even before the time when the monarchs of old were replaced by constitutional forms of government, sovereigns have had inadequate time to make clinical studies into broad areas of the counselor–regent function in management systems. Public reaction to irresponsibility and vested interests has reduced certain practices by imposing legal constraints. These initial constraints tend to be responsive to economic pressures and, up to recent times, have been less concerned with social and political conflict or control situations surrounding the director or his personal relations within the directorate.

The director system works today primarily because the board members who make up the system tacitly believe in certain unwritten axioms or laws. These beliefs are both explicit and implicit, and directors often don't know of or acknowledge that they believe in such unwritten laws. When individual directors stop to think about it, or are forced by circumstances to search for the basic issues which underlie their stewardship position, the more perceptive of them do divulge certain axiomatic beliefs and unwritten laws of management, economics, and strategy. These unwritten laws constitute a hierarchy of pragmatism overlaid on the laws and customs which envelop the director.

To try to compress director lore into scientific terms at this stage is premature and certainly too ambitious. However, a new director must consciously seek to recognize and understand these unwritten laws that are the underpinnings for the behavior patterns of the directorate. Knowledge of these unwritten laws may assist him in his career of service in this unreal world of the director; but, as Jonathan Swift wrote, "Laws are like cobwebs, which may catch small flies but let wasps and hornets break through." These unwritten laws are random and do change. Some are discarded and replaced by more modern versions; others evolve finally into explicit written laws of boardroom behavior. As Swift remarked of the mathematicians of Laputa in *Gulliver's Travels*, they were unpardonably hazy about first principles and resorted to faith, or in some cases to an uncanny sort of instinct. Faith and instinct will remain important to directors because they can sometimes be the means to penetrate the charade side of the typical directorate.

Thomas L. Hughes, president of the Carnegie Endowment for International Peace, is very much concerned about the scope of American policy and America's great twentieth century technological revolution, which, he points out, sweep across sovereignties and against walls and eat away at iron curtains. Cultural problems are immense, not only in international affairs, but certainly in the world of the manager and the director. Culture is a human problem and not a scientific one and is the child and victim of many centuries. Hughes has said, half seriously, "The twentieth century is currently made up of fourteenth-century farmers, fifteenth-century theologians, sixteenth-century politicians, seventeenth-century economists, eighteenth-century bureaucrats, nineteenth-century generals, and twenty-first century scientists." Some people, perhaps even some centuries, have a greater tendency than others for self-deception, wishful thinking, and false expectations. When we look at the mores, practices, unwritten laws, and creedal policies that shape the acts of directors today, we find it difficult to keep up with the changes. It is reported that when Adam and Eve left the garden, Eve turned to her husband and said, "Adam, we live in an age of transition." Certainly today's directors and directorates live in an age of transition and change.

Graham Claverley propounds a theory that management is a magico-religious affair resulting primarily from the fact that managers are irrational beings and that their irrationality is a survival from earlier superstitions. He also suggests that one of the best management techniques, given a choice of weapons, might be drugs and hypnosis, but they are ruled out in normal managerial circumstances. Claverley says there are few necessary ground rules beyond this one: that people are not rational creatures and their behavior is not rationally motivated even if it can be rationally explained.

This leads to a group of creedal propositions or axioms which have been collected from many sources, many from well-known personalities, others fictitious. I am especially indebted to M. F. X. Gigliotti, a good friend and former associate, for some of these "laws." All of them are widespread understandings that permeate the director's environment. They may have no basis in any written policy or communication, yet they significantly influence director and management action. The presumption in setting forth these laws calls to mind the situation that other proposers of laws faced in ancient Greece. For a time, a man proposing a law in a popular assembly did so while standing on a platform with a rope around his neck. If his law passed, they removed the rope; if it failed, they removed the platform.

ADAMS' LAW OF INEQUITY

J. Stacy Adams defines inequity and proposes what is really a theory: Inequity exists for Person whenever he perceives that the ratio of his outcomes to inputs and the ratio of Other's outcomes to Other's inputs are unequal. This may happen (1) when Person and Other are in a direct exchange relationship or (2) when both are in an exchange relationship with a third party and Person compares himself to Other. Outcomes refer to pay or job status; inputs represent the contributions brought to the job, such as age, education, and physical effort.

Adams' law of inequality.

ASHBY'S LAW OF REQUISITE VARIETY

A British neurocybernetics expert, W. Ross Ashby, states this "natural law," which is perfectly obvious once it is pointed out. The law says that control can be obtained only if the variety of the controller (and all the parts of the controller) is at least as great as the variety of the situation to be controlled. Attempted control systems that disobey this law flagrantly, and therefore do not succeed, are traffic control and control of the national economy. Management always hopes to devise systems that are simple and cheap, but often ends up having to spend large sums of money to inject the requisite variety that should have been designed into the system in the first place.

ASTOR'S LAWS OF LOSS PREVENTION

Saul D. Astor, president of Management Safeguards, Inc., New York, has five laws on loss prevention: (1) Shortages inevitably rise to the level of their budget; (2) in loss prevention, the improbable is ignored and therefore becomes probable; (3) the man you trust least can steal least; (4) effective loss prevention is always preceded by extensive losses; (5) any loss prevention control or activity tends to fail only upon being audited.

BEER'S RECURSIVE SYSTEM THEOREM

Stafford Beer, visiting professor of cybernetics at Manchester University and Business School, proposed this general theorem to validate his five-tier hierarchic model of the business firm. "If a viable system contains a viable system, then the organizational structure must be recursive." If a viable firm is organized with a five-tier (recurring) hierarchy, so is its major viable unit. If the unit is organized like this, so is its viable subunit—the individual manufacturing plant, for example. If the factory is organized like this, so is the individual viable shop unit, the section, and finally the man himself. Recursive, an adjective borrowed from the field of phonetics, means formed with an inward movement of air. In the system context, Beer implies that the threads which unite organizational theory—even if the thread is variety—constitute a general theorem saying that viable subunits of a system, such as a department, a shop, or a man, are organized in a similar way since the system is where the model came from in the first place and the subunits are formed by inward-moving forces.

BENNIS'S LAWS OF ACADEMIC PSEUDODYNAMICS

Warren Bennis, an authority on organization development and president of the University of Cincinnati, has formulated Bennis's first law of academic pseudodynamics, to wit: Routine work drives out nonroutine work, or how to smother to death all creative planning, all fundamental change in the university or in *any* institution.

Bennis's second law of academic pseudodynamics: Make whatever grand plans you will, you may be sure the unexpected or the trivial will disturb and disrupt them.

BRIGHT'S LAW OF INVENTION AND INNOVATION

Inventions usually occur before their time; or, conversely, markets are known to exist, the customers are ready to buy, but the technology or scientific state of the art is simply not there yet.

Radical innovations usually present a timing problem relative to society's readiness to accept and use. This timing problem is frequently the single most important factor in commercial success or failure, at least over the short term.

Examples of premature inventions include the Chrysler Airflow automobile, soil conditioners, coal hydrogenation, Goddard's early rocket invention, Kettering's air-cooled automo-

Bennis's law: Routine work drives out all nonroutine work,
or how to smother creativity to death.

bile engine. Examples of waiting markets include cancer cure, heart disease prevention, practical VTOL commercial aircraft.

BUTTERSIDE DOWN LAW

This law refers to the tendency of a slice of buttered bread to land butterside down when dropped. It is a pessimistic view of the way things turn out when we try to do something without thinking much about it. According to the butterside down law, such events are always adverse, and the innocent always pay the consequences. Urban blight, smog, mercuriated tuna, traffic jams, fires, thermal pollution, nuclear fallout, even inflation, war, and unreasonable fear of these so-called externalities are the results of the butterside down law.

CLARKE'S LAW

Arthur C. Clarke, science and fiction writer who suggested the first synchronous communications satellite, has hypothesized the following law: When a distinguished elderly scientist asserts that something is possible, he is almost certainly right. When he asserts that something is impossible, he is probably wrong.

COMMONER'S LAW OF INTERACTION

American scientist Barry Commoner nutshells his environmental concerns in the terse "Everything affects everything else." According to Soviet writer Aleksandr Solzhenitsyn the humanistic corollary was recently enunciated in the words, "Mankind's sole salvation lies in everyone's making everything his business." The director's corollary is that an institution's thing is everyone's thing when it is sanctioned by the trustees and by the societal environment in which the institution is permitted to exist.

COOK'S LAW: THE PROPEON RATIO

Hurley Cook's propeon ratio and its classification of members of the American Chemical Society concerns the two extremes of professional behavior. At one extreme is the 100 percent professional. In every situation he does everything right; his advice is never questioned; his recommendations are always heeded by his superiors, his peers, his subordinates, his wife and family, and all the neighbors. This description is strictly hypothetical, of course, but it serves as one end of the reference frame. At the other extreme is the 100 percent peon, who does everything wrong. His advice is never taken—or if it chances to be, he never gets credit for it. Nobody ever does anything for him—only to him. He's at the bottom of the pecking order in every conceivable situation. Again, this description is hypothetical, but the frame of reference is now complete and we can use it as a base point in developing the propeon ratio.

Our true professional status is nothing more than the ratio of the summation of all situations where we come out smelling like a PRO to the summation of all situations where we find ourselves playing the PEON role (our propeon ratio). Salary levels seem to tie in pretty well with propeon ratios, and this is logical. If your advice is considered valuable, you'll be paid well for it. Within the propeon ratio framework, the life of a peon can be a delightful experience, provided that you can afford it financially. It's the very heart of the do-your-own-thing philosophy, and it can be indulged in with abandon by those who are young or independently wealthy or don't give a damn. But acquire a wife, some kids, a car, and a home and suddenly your propeon ratio— your professional status—becomes exceedingly relevant. The goal of the American Chemical Society is to educate its members in the ways and means of raising their individual propeon ratios, according to Mr. Cook.

COPEMAN'S PRINCIPLE OF THE
SPAN OF EFFECTIVE RAPPORT

This is a modification of the classical management principle of span of control, which says that a manager cannot effectively control more than a fixed number of subordinates—generally, four to six. Subsequent management research has shown that from industry to industry the technical requirements and marketing and distribution problems are so different that no simple span-of-control principle fits all situations. Dr. George H. Copeman, British pioneer in the development of share incentive schemes who, with C. Northcote Parkinson, founded Leviathan House, replaced the principle of the span of control with the span of effective rapport. This says that the chief executive of a business should not be responsible for an organization so large that he cannot have effective rapport with all who report to him. Effective rapport involves not merely getting along well with a subordinate, but working closely enough and often enough with him to have masterminded his job and have such a level of understanding that, if the boss is away, the subordinate acts in the same ways as the boss would have acted.

CRANE'S LAW, ALSO CALLED TINSTAAFL

Called the oldest battle cry of the economics profession, Crane's Law says, "There is no such thing as a free lunch." This means you can't get something for nothing; natural resources, capital, and labor must be used in the process of producing anything of value. Just who Crane was is not clear, but Professor Nicholas Georgescu-Roegen of Vanderbilt University, a distinguished fellow of the American Economic Association, says TINSTAAFL is not nearly harsh enough. He contends that the cost of any biological or economic enterprise is always greater than the value of the product. You never get as much out of a lunch as you put into it. The explanation for this pessimistic principle is that as a rule the economic process consists in using free energy—such as coal or oil—and ultimately converting it into forms of "bound" energy, such as pollution or wastes that are no longer readily convertible into heat or mechanical power. In short, economic production is a process of downgrading the resources needed to support life.

CROSBY'S LAWS OF SITUATION MANAGEMENT

Philip Crosby, corporate vice president of International Telephone and Telegraph, has set forth ten laws which control the unflappable solver of corporate problems in managing whatever situations he gets involved in, as follows:

1 The primary concern of management is survival.

2 A person's loyalty is a function of how much he feels he is appreciated.

3 The amount of accurate information an executive possesses concerning the status of his operation varies inversely with his position in the organization.

4 The effectiveness of any program depends upon the amount of participation delegated.

5 The less systematic support a decision maker receives, the better decisions he will make.

6 Pride goes before all.

7 A job can only be as successful as the means supplied to measure it.

8 People are more important to situations than things.

9 Improvement is the only practical management goal.

10 Nobody really listens.

D'HALLUIN'S LAW OF SAFE DECENTRALIZATION

In a large organization (government or corporation), there are two equal levels of decentralization which apparently can generate the same level of management efficiency. However, only one of these levels is "safe" and is representative of sophisticated and sound management. The other level is dangerously unstable and has been the origin of many disasters stemming from uncontrolled decentralization.

This paradox can be illustrated as the classical bell-shaped (Gaussian) curve plotted against a vertical axis representing increasing management efficiency, with the horizontal axis representing increasing degree of centralization (from zero to one hundred percent) of the management function. There are two extreme situations in which the level of centralization has historically failed in the long pull: 100 percent centralization is characteristic of dictatorships, the Napoleon or Hitler style of management, and zero percent centralization is characteristic of anarchy, where there is no management and no constructive results. Experience has shown that the maximum of management efficiency and staff creativity is reached somewhere between 0 and 50 percent rather than between 50 and 100 percent centralization; that is, in the first half of the centralization process.

According to d'Halluin's law, if a bell-shaped curve is drawn starting at 0 percent efficiency and 0 percent centralization (total decentralization), the efficiency level rises rapidly as the management process is gradually centralized. Efficiency reaches a peak (theoretically 100 percent), at perhaps 25 to 35 percent centralization and then drifts off to, say, 80 percent efficiency at the halfway mark toward total centralization, ultimately reaching zero (long-term) efficiency where the dictatorship 100 percent centralization point is attained. The efficiency curve is skewed toward less than 50 percent centralization of the management process.

Thus according to this law there are two points on the curve where perhaps 80 percent efficiency is achieved, one on the upside slope and one on the downside slope of the curve. The upside slope is so steep that efficiency is particularly sensitive to a shift in degree of centralization, and thus this is a dangerous, unstable level to maintain. The downside slope of the curve is more gradual, so that maintaining organizational equilibrium at something like the 80 percent level is easier to manage; in turn, any shift in degree of centralization has less impact, positive or negative, on the resulting management efficiency.

Normal line organization behavior is to react against management attempts toward centralization, and the organizational thrust therefore tends to be from right to left toward more decentralization (and freedom). The safe decentralization point on the right-hand downside slope of the curve thus shifts toward the higher crest of the efficiency curve as management reins are relaxed. However, the unstable (equal) efficiency level on the left rising slope of the curve declines rapidly with any further move toward decentralization.

For management, it is usually easier to move an organization away from the safe level of centralization by simply relaxing controls, and for a short increment, greater efficiency and creativity are achieved as long as the shift doesn't move the organization over the hump of the curve and let it slip rapidly down the steep side. On the other hand, an organization perched at the curve's left side (unstable degree of centralization) requires a major energy push to move it up to a greater height of efficiency. In the case of governments, this might require a revolution; in the case of a corporation, a new management.

One last comment is offered by Michael d'Halluin, vice president of Arthur D. Little, Inc. (Paris), to whom acknowledgment is due for this law. The unsafe level of decentralization is really not very far from the safe level. Therefore, a decentralized management requires *more* effort to maintain an organization at the optimum level than a centralized management.

FINAGLE'S LAW

Once a job is fouled up, anything done to improve it makes it worse.

FITZ-GIBBON'S LAW

Fitz-Gibbon's law, which is attributed to Bernice Fitz-Gibbon of R. H. Macy & Company, goes like this: Creativity varies inversely with the number of cooks involved with the broth.

FYFFE'S AXIOM

An intrinsic truth postulated by Dr. Don Fyffe, psychologist and commercial supervisor for Southwestern Bell Telephone Company, Lubbock, Texas, division. It deals with the problem of defining the problem as a first step in finding a solution. Fyffe's axiom: The problem-solving process will always break down at the point at which it is possible to determine who caused the problem. Fyffe considers the phenomenon part of the "why hierarchy," which is used extensively in industry, education, and government as a direct result of childhood conditioning on "why" type questioning, the final answer to which winds up in a "because." The attempts are to fix blame and find the culprit rather than find the solution. Ultimately, the corporate resolution of a problem rests on acceptance of the validity of this axiom according to Fyffe. If corporations do not seek positive measures to correct the problem rather than fix blame, the axiom goes into play and the problem is insoluble.

GG'S LAW

GG's law, as propounded by Guy Goden, says that generalizedness of incompetence is directly proportional to highestness in the hierarchy.

GIANNINO'S LAW OF WORK

Effective work is contrary to the interests of society because most people, when confronted with the need to take action, take the wrong action. Many directors and executives survive on this principle, particularly nonexecutive directors. This is not to suggest that they do not work, for they may work very hard. But if a man is to do effective work, he must make decisions; and if he makes wrong decisions, he's in trouble. If he works without making decisions, he usually is on safe ground; thus Giannino's law of work.

By way of elaboration, the angel is the ideal nonexecutive director because all its decisions are taken on high and are of course correct. Most people spend their lives unconsciously avoiding decisions. Otherwise they risk martyrdom, and martyrs are accepted only when dead. When alive, they are making unpopular decisions. Hence the avoidance of decision is effective from the standpoint of Giannino's law of work.

GREENBERG'S FIRST LAW OF EXPERTISE

Daniel S. Greenberg, Washington editor of *Saturday Review Science,* postulates this law of expertise: Don't ask the barber whether you need a haircut.

The corollary of this is: The creators of a technology constitute the worst possible source of advice as to whether it should be utilized.

Greenberg cites this case in point. Toward the end of World War II Secretary of War Henry L. Stimson asked the

Greenberg's first law of expertise: Don't ask the barber whether you need a haircut.

leaders of the atom bomb project whether their creation should be used. The question came at the end of a four-year, around-the-clock effort to build the bomb, and they naturally said yes. From this episode Greenberg draws a further principle: Not only should the technical leaders be excluded from making any decision regarding the use of their creation, but their sponsors should also be excluded from conjuring up outside advice. Interpreting Greenberg's first law of expertise for the boardroom, the expert who has the least to gain from a proposition at hand should be heeded most.

GRESHAM'S LAW

Sir Thomas Gresham, sixteenth century English financier, is famous for his law: When two items of the same face value have different intrinsic values, the lesser will stay in circulation and the greater will be hoarded or exported. In other words, bad money drives out good.

GUMMIDGE'S LAW

The credited amount of expertise varies in inverse proportion to the number of statements understood by the general public.

GUMPERSON'S LAW

According to Gumperson's law, the contradictory of a welcome probability will assert itself whenever such an eventuality is likely to be most frustrating; in other words, the good parking places are always on the other side of the street.

HELLER'S TRUTHS OF MANAGEMENT

Robert Heller, British journalist, currently editor of *Management Today* and formerly with the *Financial Times* and *The Observer,* has developed a series of ten laws which he calls truths of management or an anti-myth kit. His thesis is that management, which is a general human activity, is guided not by management textbooks but by history, sociology, and psychology. Heller says the prime myth of management—that it exists—seeks to take management away from where it belongs and to put it on a pedestal of pseudoscience. He suggests that if his ten truths do not keep one off the pedestal, they will at least make the drop shorter. These are his laws:

1 Think before you act: the money isn't yours.

2 No manager ever devotes effort to proving himself wrong.

3 All good management is merely an expression of one great idea.

4 Cash in must exceed cash out.

5 However high the level, management capability is always less than the organization needs.

6 Either a manager is competent to run the business, or he is not.

7 If you need sophisticated calculations to justify an action, it is probably wrong.

8 If you're doing something wrong, you'll do it badly.

9 If you are attempting the impossible, you are bound to fail.

10 The easiest way of making money is to stop losing it.

HUBBARD'S DOCTRINE OF THE STABLE DATUM

Scientologist–philosopher–author L. Ron Hubbard posits this doctrine as an aid to navigation "when all difficulties are fundamentally confusions." Confusion is defined as any set of factors or circumstances which do not seem to have an immediate solution. To untangle such a maze of motion, the doctrine of the stable datum is suggested, and this can be applicable to some boardroom situations.

"A confusion is only a confusion so long as *all* particles are in motion. As long as no one factor in a situation is clearly defined or understood, confusion will reign." No matter how great or complex, all confusing situations are composed of data and factors. "Grasp one piece and locate it thoroughly. Stop the motion of this piece, and see how other pieces function in relation to it. In this way confusion becomes steadied, and soon the situation can be mastered in its entirety."

When confronted with an overcomplicated situation, the stable datum approach is to adopt one item of fact, even if it is not true. All that matters is that you adopt a stable datum so that you can look at other data in relation to it, align the data, and sort out the confusion. If the stable datum is shaken, invalidated, or disproved, you are right back where you started: in the midst of confusion. But as long as you have the tools, you can repair the damage by adopting a new stable datum or putting the old one back in place.

Mastery over confusion, says Hubbard, puts ideals such as certainty and security within reach. To achieve order out of confusion is to achieve control. Much control is uncertain, stupid. There is bad control, but there is also good control. The difference is that good control is certain, positive, predictable; bad control is uncertain, variable, unpredictable. Control is necessary to bring order out of a confusing situation.

HULL'S LAW

This theorem postulates that the combined pull of several patrons is the sum of their separate pulls multiplied by the number of patrons. Pull is defined as an employee's relationship by blood, marriage, or acquaintance with the person above him in the hierarchy. A patron is a person above you in the hierarchy who can help you to rise. The combined pull of several patrons has a multiplication effect because the patrons talk among themselves and constantly reinforce one another's opinions of your merits and their determination to do something for you. With a single patron you get none of this reinforcement. "Many a patron makes a promotion."

HYMER'S LAWS OF ECONOMIC DEVELOPMENT

Stephan Hymer, the economist, has argued that contemporary international relations are rapidly being reshaped by two laws of economic development, the law of increasing firm size and the law of uneven development. The law of increasing firm size says that, since the Industrial Revolution, firms have tended to increase in size from the workshop to the factory to the national corporation to the multidivisional corporation and now to the multinational corporation. The law of uneven development says that the international economy tends to produce poverty as well as wealth, underdevelopment as well as development.

JAMES'S LAW OF IGNORANCE

Denis James, British author of *The Bluffer's Guidebook* series, cites this law: The time it takes for a clever man to influence a stupid man is inversely proportionate to the gap in their knowledge. In other words, if a board is meeting to approve a scheme which has been carefully studied by the staff, and if the staff's lengthy report is full of economic appraisals, lengthy formulas, integral signs, and uncompromising recommendations, the board members will not wish to exhibit their ignorance by asking questions that may already be answered in the report. So there will be wise looks and rapid agreement. Conversely, if a discussion centers around the purchase of a new company car, the color of the corporate jet, or a change in the interior decoration of the boardroom, the discussion can last a long time. There is of course an inverse relationship between the amount of money involved and the length of the discussion. The greater the amount of money, the quicker the decision.

JULIAN'S LAW

"Ethics in international engineering is in inverse proportion to the need for work." Corollaries to the law are many and diverse. For example, as a firm's backlog of foreign business diminishes, so does its ethical sensitivity; its ethics increase in direct proportion to the foreign workload. Perhaps "fat cats breed ethics" might be most descriptive of, if not quite as lofty in language as, Julian's law. It is said that during the construction of the Appian Way the imperial Roman project manager, Julius Julian III, was confronted with many solicitations from out-of-town consulting engineers seeking work. This made him observe that in general the more substantial the firm, the less the deviation from ethical standards. His proposition has since been restated as Julian's law.

KEMMER'S LAW

An antitrust law rule-of-thumb, "If it works, it is illegal," was humorously postulated by Sherman J. Kemmer, former president of the Licensing Executives Society, an international licensing organization. This law is a gibe at the complex antitrust law interpretations and case law that have been developing around the international licensing of product and process technology and know-how.

Kemmer's law shows licensing to be a difficult task of threading through the constraints and the conflicting attitudes and interpretations as to the legal way of doing business with industrial property rights. Antitrust clearance is often doomed even though the licensing satisfies a long-felt need.

LANE TRACY'S NATURAL LAWS OF AUTHORITY

Lane Tracy has set forth two natural laws of authority as helpful in understanding the difference between the vertical and horizontal hierarchies in organizations.

1. In its free state, authority is a lighter-than-air gas. When introduced into an air-breathing vertical organization, gaseous authority tends to rise to the top of the organization and expand, producing a structural arrangement in which the buoyancy of gaseous authority lends stability to this top-heavy structure.

2. If allowed to remain in one position for any length of time, authority crystallizes into a hard, rodlike substance called formal or bureaucratic authority. The crystalline form of authority adds strength to the structure, but also reduces its buoyancy.

MASON HAIRE'S LAW OF GROWTH OF INTEGRATING AND CONTACT FUNCTIONS

Mason Haire's quantification of Parkinson's law says that within a three-dimensional sphere (a total firm), if size doubles, contact functions grow like the sphere (a fourfold increase) and internal integrating functions grow like the volume of the sphere (an eightfold increase in firm size). Note that the ultimate objectives and decisions remain centralized. Mason Haire, a well-known industrial psychologist, is Professor of Management at the Alfred P. Sloan School of Massachusetts Institute of Technology.

MASON HAIRE'S LAW OF THE SITUATION

This law concerns the confusing and persistent concept that there is a clear-cut distinction between line and staff, which runs sharply counter to the notion that responsibility is commensurate with authority. Implicit in the concept that line is distinct from staff is the view—or caricature—that line authority is ultimately rooted in ownership, vested in the CEO through the board of directors, and passed down the line. The staff man's expertise exerts authority, according to this caricature, by means of persuasion, indirection, and advice.

The authority of the line man is becoming more like that of the staff man each day, as the line man's authority is drawn away from ownership and he becomes a professional manager dominated by the law of the situation, the imperatives of the science of management, and the compelling logic of what must be done. The law of the situation puts it that the authority is moving into the process itself, as one man tells another to do something because that is the appropriate thing to do under the circumstances.

MAUSS'S LAW

This law was formulated by a French sociologist who was eventually driven insane by his researches into human behavior. It explains that, if income tax had not already been necessitated by government, it would have been invented to satisfy consumer demand.

MEYER'S LAWS OF ADVERTISING

Alan H. Meyer of Glenn Advertising, Inc., Dallas, Texas, some time ago postulated the following ten laws of advertising and marketing:

Mauss's law: If income tax had not already been necessitated, it would have been invented.

1 Bad shops tend to get worse and good ones better.

2 The name acquires the attribute of the thing, not vice versa.

3 Years on the job have little to do with experience.

4 The youthful viewpoint has little to do with age.

5 Any bright tyro can write a great national campaign; only an old pro can write a good brochure.

6 The less able a person is to create advertising himself, the more likely he is to make changes in art or copy if he has the authority to do so.

7 Secure people share credit; insecure people steal it.

8 Doubling the workload does not double the work.

9 It is better to work for a smart son-of-a-bitch than for a dumb son-of-a-bitch.

10 The best ad is a good product.

MURPHY'S LAW

This law has many variations, but they all stem from one axiom: You can't win. Seven versions are—

1 Nothing you do, however brilliantly conceived and executed, will ever satisfy more than 5 percent of the people concerned.

2 It is easier to get involved in something than to get out of it.

3 If you fool around with something long enough, it will break.

4 If you can keep calm and collected while everyone else is confused and panic-stricken, you just don't understand what's going on.

5 If at first you don't succeed, give up.

6 The prevailing situation cannot improve; it can only go on getting steadily worse.

7 If something can go wrong, it will.

A unit quantum of randomness is called a murph in honor of Murphy's law.

VARIATIONS ON THE LAW OF EDSEL MURPHY

Edsel Murphy, who developed one of the most profound concepts of the twentieth century, is practically unknown to most engineers. He is a victim of his own law. He seemed destined for a secure place in the engineering Hall of Fame, but something went wrong. His real contribution lay not merely in the discovery of the law, but more in its universality and its impact. The law itself, though inherently simple, has formed a foundation on which future generations will build. In fact, the law first came to him in all its simplicity when his bride-to-be informed him of the impending birth of an heir to the family fortune.

1 Dimensions will always be expressed in the least usable term. Velocity, for example, will be expressed in furlongs per fortnight.

2 A device selected at random from a group having 99 percent reliability will be a member of the 1 percent group.

3 Any wire cut to length will be too short.

4 The necessity of making a major design change increases as the fabrication of the system approaches completion.

5 In any given price estimate, cost of equipment will exceed estimate by a factor of 3.

6 After the last of 16 mounting screws has been removed from an access cover, it will be discovered that the wrong access cover has been removed.

7 After an access cover has been secured by 16 hold-down screws, it will be discovered that the gasket has been omitted.

8 A patent application will be preceded by one week by a similar application made by an independent worker.

9 If a project requires n components, there will be $n - 1$ units in stock.

10 A dropped tool will land where it can do the most damage. Also known as the law of selective gravitation.

11 The probability that a dimension will be omitted from a plan or drawing is directly proportional to its importance.

12 If a prototype functions perfectly, subsequent production units will malfunction.

13 Components that must not and cannot be assembled improperly will be.

14 The most delicate component will drop.

PACIFICO'S LAW OF HUMAN RELATIVITY

Carl Pacifico, president of Management Supplements, Inc., revealed his law in a luncheon speech before the 1968 Chemical Industry Association's annual president's luncheon in New York City. Adapted from Einstein, the law underlies almost all person-to-person contact in a top-flight mismanaged business. According to Mr. Pacifico, the law of human relativity is, "To the extent that I diminish you, then relatively I advance."

Mr. Pacifico suggests the relevance of the law in references to the size of the mismanaged market and further supports his finding that in the absence of an outside force, such as a new competitor, a company can tolerate extensive internal incompetence without serious effect.

PADDY O'NEIL-DUNNE'S RULES FOR BUSINESS GAMBLERS

Paddy O'Neil-Dunne, in his mid-sixties, has disengaged from his career in the British tobacco world—he was an international director of Rothman's—to spend more time on his beloved roulette wheel, including writing a book on roulette for the millions. He argues that a gambler's instinct is invaluable in making unusual successes out of ordinary business situations and has drawn up a set of rules. The four that follow are the pertinent ones for a director:

1. A tight budget brings out the best creative instincts in a man. Give him unlimited funds, and it is incredible how he finds ways of squandering money on wasteful pursuits.

2. There can be but one boss, and he must avoid compromise. O'Neil-Dunne argues that the Russians have the best system in that the real embassy boss is seldom seen, carries no title, and devotes himself to running the embassy, while all the

Western ambassadors are wearing themselves out at cocktail parties.

3. Declare war on managerial ego. Install round tables in your boardroom and executives' canteen; address notices and memos in alphabetical order; avoid fancy titles; describe job functions; cut out special-quality stationery for the boss and his entourage; eliminate reserved parking areas, buzzers, and private lavatories. The company transport should be standard utility cars for all.

4. When you find yourself in a Rolls, being driven by a liveried chauffeur at the shareholders' expense, it's time to retire.

PAGE'S LAW OF EXECUTIVE INSOLVENCY

According to Page's law, a raise in salary, however impressive, is rarely adequate to cover existing financial obligations despite stringent family economy campaigns and self-denial in personal spending. (See Mauss's law.)

THE PARETO PRINCIPLE

Vilfredo Pareto was a nineteenth century Italian economist whose principle explains practically everything about business. Roughly speaking, the Pareto principle says that 20 percent of the facts are critical to 80 percent of the outcome. If you have these facts, it is absurd to wait for more. The hunger for complete data is "paralysis by analysis." To apply this law further, 20 percent of the customers account for 80 percent of the turnover, and 20 percent of the components account for 80 percent of the cost of the finished product.

PARKINSON'S LAWS

C. Northcote Parkinson's first law is the most famous one to bear his name, but he has enunciated a number of others as well. Here are five of Parkinson's laws.

Parkinson's first law: Work expands so as to fill the time available for its completion.

Parkinson's second law: Expenditure rises to meet income.

Parkinson's third law: Expansion means complexity, and complexity, decay; or, to put it even more plainly—the more complex, the sooner dead.

Parkinson's law of levity: This is the law by which the suitably gifted (or guided) individual rises to the top of the organization chart. Contrasted with this is the law of gravity, which holds other people down.

Parkinson's law of delay: Delay is the deadliest form of denial with mathematical formulae to display it.

THE PETER PRINCIPLE

Laurence F. Peter is the author of the Peter principle, which says that in a hierarchy every employee tends to rise to his level of incompetence. Peter's corollary states that in time, every post tends to be occupied by an employee who is incompetent to carry out its duties. Work is accomplished by those employees who have not yet reached their level of incompetence.

PIET HEIN'S FIRST LAW OF BUDGETING

If you want to know where your money went, you must spend it quickly, before it's spent.

THE PINOCCHIO PRINCIPLE

This principle is Professor Kenneth E. Boulding's expression for organizational behavior associated with the budding process, whereby an organization comes into being in a manner corresponding to asexual reproduction in biology. A church forms a college to educate its adherents and propagate its doctrines; a corporation forms a subsidiary to focus on one aspect of its business; a country establishes a colony as Britain did in America. Then the budding operation comes into play, as expressed in Boulding's Pinocchio principle; the thing that has been set up is supposed to be a puppet, but it starts to walk by itself. The church-founded college begins to behave like an independent college, then eventually breaks its church connection and becomes independent in fact. The corporate subsidiary takes off on its own, buys itself from the mother company, and becomes an independent corporate entity. The colony has a revolution and becomes an independent nation.

RENFREW'S LAW

Dr. Renfrew, a public relations officer at Stevens Institute in Hoboken, New Jersey, has formulated the following law:

1 The amount of publicity is inversely proportional to the number of releases.

2 Management evaluation of public relations effectiveness is based on number of releases.

3 Therefore, most press releases are designed for interoffice distribution.

RUDIN'S LAW

In a crisis that forces a choice among alternative courses of action, most people will make the worst possible choice.

SCHWARTZ'S LAW

If something can go right, it will. This is a counter law to Murphy's law.

SHANAHAM'S LAW

The length of a meeting rises with the square of the number of people present.

SNOW'S LAW

C. P. Snow, in his *Science and Government,* reported on the feud between two prominent English scientists who were advisers to the British government during World War II, Sir Henry Tizard and F. A. Lindemann. This account sets forth what is called Snow's law. The first part is, as he terms it, "banal." "If you are going to have a scientist in a position of isolated power, the only scientist among non-scientists, it's dangerous when he has bad judgment." The second part doesn't shout quite so loud: "If you are going to have a scientist in a position of isolated power, the only scientist among non-scientists, it is dangerous whoever he is." This was a lesson which burned itself in on many people during the controversies of Tizard and Lindemann in 1939 and 1945. "Whoever he is, whether he is the wisest scientist in the world, we must never tolerate a scientific overlord again."

TROWBRIDGE'S FIVE BASIC LAWS OF CRISIS MANAGEMENT
Martin Trowbridge, managing director of Pennwalt International, a British-based subsidiary of Pennwalt Corporation, U.S. chemicals and pharmaceuticals group, has suggested that businessmen dream of a crisis-free world. Crises involve two essential elements: threat and time pressure. Indeed, the temperature of a crisis depends more on the time scale than on the magnitude of the threat. Business problems may be confined to controllable proportions if executives keep in mind five basic laws of crisis management:

1 Lengthen the time scale and the crisis becomes more manageable.

2 If possible, get someone else to manage your crisis, or try to see it through the eyes of an uninvolved spectator.

3 Don't overreact.

4 Before acting, decide whether the crisis will get better or worse, if nothing is done about it.

5 Beware of the manager who is too good at managing crises; he will ensure that you live in a perpetual state of chaos.

Trowbridge's fifth law: Beware of the manager who is
too good at managing crises.

WEIL'S LAW

Professor André Weil is a member of the School of Mathematics at The Institute for Advanced Study, Princeton, New Jersey. His colleagues quote Weil's law, which he has formulated, as follows: "The first-rate man will try to surround himself with his equals, or betters if possible. The second-rate man will surround himself with third-rate men. The third-rate man will surround himself with fifth-rate men."

WICKER'S LAW

Tom Wicker of *The New York Times* has postulated that "government expands to absorb revenue—and then some."

12 The Directorate: Corporate-Centric or Synarchy?

The charm and the paradox of the American economy is its external symmetry which conceals those millions and millions of decisions made daily. . . . These individual decisions . . . involve related issues of aesthetics and ethics, of psychology and philosophy. What to make, what to charge, and how to market the wares are questions that embrace moral as well as economic questions. The answers are conditioned by the personal value system of the decision maker and the institutional values which affect the relationships of the individual to the community.

The strength and vitality of Western economies are largely attributable to the evolution and behavior of the corporate form of organization. In its earliest development and until recently, the corporate structure's major strength was its ability to marshal resources and to apply them with discrimination to the attainment of limited economic objectives. This pattern of behavior is focused inward; it is *corporate-centric*.

In the late 1800s and early 1900s a corporation's primary objective was to maximize the owners' interests, usually on a short-term basis. Since the early 1900s the economic interests of corporations have broadened to include the interests of suppliers, customers, employees, and hired managers. In the early years, as corporate organizations grew in size and in economic power, the community reacted by enacting legislation to limit or modify the growth and power of these organizations. Among the laws designed to limit the economic power of any one organization in a definable geographical area, or producing a given product or dealing with a specific market, were the Sherman Antitrust Act and the Clayton Act. Among the laws designed to protect working people from the adverse use of corporate power were the Norris-LaGuardia Act and the Railway Labor Act.

Corporate power has at least two relationships. One relationship is individual, as when an institution is capable of affecting other individuals or groups. The second relationship is societal and is effective in determining how the particular power base relates to the surrounding social-political structure.

The growth of unionism in the United States and in other industrialized countries was a social response to the great economic power of corporations in the context of their individual power relationship. The efforts to curb the influence and strength of corporations by the community (through its elected representatives) and by labor (through its legally protected rights to organize and to bargain) served to restrict the extreme instances of corporate-centric behavior in the United States and other Western nations, as it relates to employee groups. Legislative control also contributed to the development of more socially responsible corporate programs for safe working conditions, greater guarantees of product safety, and the employment and training of minority group workers and other handicapped or penalized workers.

Recently the significance of environmental pollution has focused local and national government and industry attention on solving problems caused by polluting factories, disposal centers, and careless public practices. This reaction to the use of power is concerned with extra-organizational matters and relationships in the environmental, social, and political context. Some corporations seem to drag their feet and need the prodding of legislative action before they take steps to correct problems affecting environmental and social welfare. Sometimes regulation or legislation is necessary also to allow companies to compete on a fair basis. However, many corporations, having learned from the past, have been striving to anticipate these redefinitions of the corporate role and mission in society so that they can better serve their communities and thereby make regulatory and legislative approaches less necessary.

If we examine the record up to now, we see clearly that the corporate form of collective action in governing the productive relationships of men with one another and with the physical environment has served us well. This form and function has been generally sufficient for the growth of the institution whose production goals have been the primary objectives. The frame of reference has been the standard of living from an economic point of view.

The challenge to the very nature of this form and function of the corporation is raised by the changing concepts of man and his relationships with society and the environment. Institutional objectives are changing as there is further differentiation and specialization. The main propulsive force of the business corporation is shifting from the production of goods to the production of services. These services perform a variety of functions which are associated with the qualitative aspects of living and are co-determining factors in a new frame of reference where political, social, and economic change is rapid.

It is now popular to wear a badge of concern for the quality of life, and this phrase usually travels with a companion phrase, reallocation of resources. Assessments of the quality of life and the measures needed to reallocate resources are mostly subjective and should be of prime concern to directors who must determine courses of action and general guidelines for the institution.

What does all this mean for the directorate? How do such subjective developments actually influence the composition and functioning of a board of directors? Will these pressures lead to new forms of corporate organization and to new patterns of private corporate behavior and control? The answer to this last question seems to be yes. The shift in our values toward greater concern for continuing education, recreation, environmental quality, and personal freedom presages a change in the nature of all institutions. No longer can a board of directors decide that the direction and sole objective of the business corporation is the economic production of goods or services because its activity increasingly affects other sectors of human affairs. Recognition of the need to serve other concordant objectives for the long run must be part of the calculus which the board of directors uses in making its determinations.

In the past a corporation and its directorate could be single-purposed in orientation, concentrating on limited economic advantages. But this is no longer true. Directorates in the past could consist almost exclusively of persons who represented specific economic interests important for corporate performance. The primary legal basis for the decisions of such boards was to further the interests of the owners they represented. As for the community at large, a board needed to consider the community's interests only insofar as it was legally liable to do so. Obviously, some far-seeing boards have moved well beyond this limited definition of their responsibilities and are becoming socially engaged.

Forecasting the changing nature, form, and function of the corporate organization has become a "growth industry" in itself, with a bandwagon of economists, sociologists, scientists, journalists, futurists, consultants, and politicians. However, few businessmen, and few directorates, have effectively tackled this complex subject. Beyond preoccupation with other things, the main reason is the lack of a mature theory of the corporation as an institution in a dynamic context of conflict, tension, trade-offs, and competition by political economics and different value systems.

The boardroom is, or should be, the focal point for many of these institutional reactions to public, natural, and competitive forces and for the development of strategies to cope with them. And properly so, because as a rule the actions required entail major changes in concept, purpose, and policy. Product performance standards and guarantees, capital for environmental management and safety, support level for and nature of defense research, and social programs are increasingly important considerations that determine corporate activities. Directorates must modify their past corporate-centric posture and find ways to address these changes. Some alterations appear to be required in the form and function of the directorate so as to make it better able to cope with multiple objectives.

Reactions to Change

As circumstances have changed and external pressures have increased, boards of directors have reacted in predictable ways. The first response is understandably an adaptive one. The boards strive to cope with extra-organizational social and environmental forces by taking steps to placate the threatening factions. When there have been significant pressure groups with sufficient power to cause economic harm, corporations have been

This practice is manifest in the election of a minority group director, an educator, an environmentalist, a youth representative...

inclined to add representatives of such factions to their boards so that the points of view and attitudes of these factions could be considered in decision making. This practice is manifest in the election of a minority group director, an educator, an environmentalist, a youth or student representative, and so on. While the practice has been labeled tokenism by some critics, it is useful because it provides varied inputs, expertise, advice, and counsel. Whether these added director inputs are effective depends on two things: the individual's expertness on subjects of concern to the board and his persuasive abilities. The value of diverse points of view on a board is limited because directors are captives and have no power base other than their own expertness in subjects that are of concern to a particular corporate board. Most directors are selected and invited to stand for election to the board by the enthroned directors. The shareowners rarely contest such choices when the time comes to ratify them.

The acquisition of consultative directors is an adaptive response to the necessity for dealing with change. Recent elections of financial or business professionals as trustees on hospital boards are good examples. A hospital can become so large and complicated in its efforts to provide the best health care that soaring expenses threaten survival, and the crisis demands a critical cost–benefit examination as well as management control. Yet the power leverage of these added directors is usually one of influencing decisions through expertise in, say, cost–benefit analysis rather than one of using a veto to control decisions.

While few corporations have voluntarily given board membership and significant power to the representatives of other claimants on corporate resources and potential, some countries have legislative requirements that such groups be represented, as discussed in Chapter 4. In Germany, for example, the requirement of co-determination gives substantial power, but not yet controlling influence, to representatives of employee groups. It is compulsory in certain German industries to have a two-tier board. Under this system the executive board is supplemented with a supervisory board composed of an equal number of representatives of shareowners, trade unions and employees, and management. If voting is deadlocked, an additional board member, agreed to by the co-determining parties, makes the final decision.

This co-determination differs from the consultative director concept in that the representatives of the trade unions and the employees do have a power base from which to exert their influence.

In many Western countries, including the United States, there has been the beginning of a movement to require that community and public interests be represented on boards of directors. Particularly in the cases of quasi-public corporations, major groups that are interested in or affected by the activities of these corporations are being given board positions and opportunities to influence, if not control, the course of corporate affairs. COMSAT is one recent case in point.

COMSAT—an acronym for Communications Satellite Corporation—was organized in the United States in 1963 as a recognized monopoly that would build and run a commercial communications system in conjunction and cooperation with other countries. The Communications Satellite Act of 1962 provided for the establishment of the U.S. portion of the global satellite system, subject to federal legislation. Half the initial $200 million stock issue was purchased by communications common carriers and half by the general public. Public directors appointed by the President replaced the incorporators once the stock was sold.

COMSAT's directorate, which is partly consultative and partly co-determinative, is composed of industrialists, educators, lawyers, a labor leader, and communications industry representatives. However, in its public function COMSAT serves two major power groups: private industrial companies in the communications business and the federal government—both dedicated to regulating and improving certain worldwide communications. The board of directors determines corporate direction and resolves conflicts. Public shareownership adds an economic dimension for the benefit of optional investors.

The trend is toward public–private corporations (AMTRAK, the U.S. Postal Corporation, The Port of New York Authority), and a stronger movement in this direction can be anticipated. Sometimes these institutions may be formed because government or industry alone has failed to do an effective job, sometimes because a joint undertaking makes for a more effective product or service. Each of these quasi-governmental corporations has a single overriding objective, and the constituency and the board of directors are focused on fulfilling this single purpose.

Another form of structure and power-sharing which may well find increased use involves joint rule or control over major corporate efforts where clearly there are multiple objectives. This form resembles an oligarchy; its ruling group consists of a number of factions, each with an independent power base and each with different objectives and different time horizons. Recent examples of such a form of oligarchy are the Eastman Pond Project near Hanover, New Hampshire, and ADELA.

The Controlled Environment Corporation of New Hampshire is concerned with the development of the Eastman Pond Project, a 4,000-acre area in the mountain and lake region south of Dartmouth College. The constituency and the ownership structure of this enterprise are noteworthy. Dartmouth College and the Manchester Bank and Trust Company of New Hampshire each own one-third. The Society for the Preservation of Forests of New Hampshire and the United Life and Accident Insurance Company of New Hampshire each own one-sixth. The objectives of this Eastman Pond development are at least threefold. The obvious first objective is ecological: to protect the area for recreation and living conditions, for wildlife, and for the preservation of natural resources. The second objective is educational: an experimental laboratory for Dartmouth's business and ecological development projects. The third objective, not insignificant, is economic gain from the appropriate sale of property, including planned communities and recreational areas. Eastman Pond, for all the institutions involved, is a part of their investment portfolios; and they fully expect a good return on that investment.

ADELA—Atlantic Community Development Group for Latin America—a private development organization and minority investor, also has synarchical overtones, for it has multipronged objectives. ADELA provides money, know-how, and management for nurturing Latin American private enterprise activities, which give it a commonality of purpose. It has a multifaceted emphasis on social, educational, economic, and managerial development rather than merely on technological or economic development in this area. The associated institutions which sponsor and direct ADELA are financial, professional, and industrial; their separate purposes tend to be primarily economic, but, for self-interest as well as societal interests, they combine their powers to direct and serve ADELA's multiple economic and social objectives. Organized in 1963, ADELA has helped mobilize more than $2.1 billion in new venture investment. For every dollar invested by ADELA, at least $9 is invested by banks, lending institutions, and other companies. Some of the largest banks and industrial companies in the United States, Canada, Europe, Japan, and Latin America—239 in all—back ADELA with technical and managerial know-how; and each has subscribed up to $500,000.

In 1972 there were 113 directors on the board of ADELA Investment Company, S.A. (incorporated in Luxembourg). These directors, who represented banks, industrial companies, law firms, and insurance companies, had the stewardship of more than $300 million in fulfilling ADELA's purposes as a private development organization and a minority investor in Latin America. The socioeconomic imbalances and pressures in Latin America, including education and training of people, are addressed by ADELA through its primary function of increasing economic impact—and doing it at a profit, which is considered essential for the growth, diversity, and continuity of all facets of private enterprise.

A Form of Synarchy

As can be seen in the Eastman Pond Project and ADELA examples, the directors in a joint-rule undertaking represent different factions and have different, albeit harmonious, interests in its activities. Their long-term interests are concordant, and their objectives are congruent and mutually reinforcing. Each participant, however, also has an independent power base. This is why the term synarchy is suggested, since it involves conjoint rule of the enterprise that has differentiated objectives and differing time horizons.

While this pattern of board composition and behavior is not yet widespread, given the complexity of present-day corporate institutions and society at large, it is reasonable to expect that more and more institutions of this nature will be formed in the future. It would be helpful, therefore, to compare synarchical types of institutions with the traditional forms of organization.

An idealized synarchical model would have differentiated, associated, congruent, and phased objectives. Its mode of functioning tends to be a syndicated effort in which associations with other institutions are officially authorized in order to undertake joint tasks and to negotiate positions on heterogeneous activities which concern them all. Legal complications aside, there should be an opportunity for joint determination and pursuit of multiple yet concordant goals between institutions whose primary purposes are different, but whose secondary and long-term interests are harmonious.

If the societal and environmental framework is considered as the overall system within which institutions function, a comparison of two organizational models might look like the accompanying listing.

Systems Attributes	Institutional Organization Models and Style	
	Corporate-Centric	Synarchical
Concept	Single-focus stewardship and management. Usually with a primary simple charter and objective. Rational.	Bifocal stewardship and management. Multipurpose under a broad charter. High political and social content. May have irrational or arational components.
Structure	Normally closed, stable, formal, simplistic, hierarchic.	More open, adaptive, organic, complex.
Critical size	Can be small, medium, or large.	Usually involves larger diverse entities.
Constituency	Relatively homogeneous, defined composition, stable ownership with single interests. Trusteeship associated with ownership, employees, and "hired" advisers.	Amalgam or coalition of members or owners with heterogeneous interests. Trusteeship not necessarily associated with ownership, rather with extra-organizational interests.
Directorial/managerial	Top-down sovereignty, tends to unilateral style, limited scope of trusteeship.	Co-opting of trustees, often multipurpose directions, systems sensitivity.

Systems
Attributes   **Institutional Organization Models and Style**

Performance	Corporate-Centric	Synarchical
General	Monolithic, monarchical, normally resists change.	Associational, coalitional, seeks optimum change.
Predictability	Certain, determinate, normal risks taken.	Uncertain, indeterminate risks.
Parameters	Measures achievement against self-serving criteria, especially profit and deviations from plan, policy, or budget. Tactical and strategic approaches. Inward focus.	Evaluated by external responses, market value, social benefits, reputation, and new values sought. Potentiality is the measure. Outward focus.
Social	Somewhat restricted, tends to be a secondary purpose.	Broader interests, clearly socially beneficial and often multipurpose.
Objectives		
Organizational goals	Usually focused on productivity, efficiency, stability, continuity; evolutionary mode.	Innovational, useful change based on value judgments, sometimes discontinuous or revolutionary.
Time horizon	Unlimited but often short-range perspective.	Limitless, longer-range perspective.
Future outlook	Backward-looking. Actuality and capability are the parameters; optimum allocation of available resources.	What ought to be possible by realizing all opportunities. Establishes new norms; may require new resources.

The issue at hand is how much the growth of modern organizations makes achievement more complicated. As in biological growth, increases in differentiation and specialization are attended by shifts in relationships between institutions, their directors, and those who are influenced by them. Undoubtedly, future corporate structure will be affected in different degrees and at different levels.

Systems Viewpoint

It is to cope with change that we resort to systems thinking, which is by no means a new concept. In the fifteenth century Nicholas of Cusa postulated the systems notion (*coincidentia oppositorum*) that freedom among the parts of a whole, and freedom as to which parts are in opposition to each other, nevertheless forms a higher-order unity. Under this concept a single-minded corporate-centric director who has trusteeship over one institution must accept its struggle against other institutions and the interests of the total community system as a positive factor leading toward a higher order of attainment. In time this conflict theory should become culturally legitimate at the trustee level of institutions. The executive, administrative, and operating levels will remain concerned in decreasing degree with such a philosophy of existence. Their job remains focused on the primary purpose of their organization, leaving them less time to deal with secondary purposes and the impact of the institution on the outside world.

In coping with change and serving multiple objectives, just how far an institution in one sector of activity can go in formally interlocking its directors with institutions in other spheres is a practical problem that requires a case-by-case decision. Consultation is the current adaptive response, co-determination is a reality in Western Europe, and there is increasing clamor in the United States for public and labor representation on boards of directors. The few examples of the synarchical model for directorate organization are intriguing, if speculative, indications of another institutional means of handling future change and future demands.

Undoubtedly the organizational models will blend

Multiple objectives.

and form mutations. Certainly, synarchy does not fit all situations. Individual directors must decide on their own, however, when it is prudent to lend their respective talents, understanding, and interests to the service of the respective institutions.

This capsule view of what appears to be an emerging trend in the composition and behavior of boards of directors shows the flexibility of the corporate form and the ability of corporations to adapt to the environment in which they exist and of which they are important and powerful members. It should be a challenge to all directors to review the scope and organizational model of each directorate and to question whether it can reach anything like its potential. The greater spectrum of purpose and the variety of organizational models which can cope with multiple objectives may well lead to greater achievement and longer life for each institution and a more valuable service rendered by individual directors.

13 Boardspeak and Buzzwords

Dr. Maximillian Schubart, German industrial management consultant, has opined, "The higher you climb in the business hierarchy, the less you need to know. If you aim at being a director you must be careful to avoid knowing anything at all. What is needed at the top is not knowledge but flair." Dr. Schubart exaggerates a bit, but there is no question that flair is a useful attribute. One practice that requires flair has crept into boardrooms of late: the use of buzzwords from the management sciences and other professional and commercial realms.

Anyone can acquire knowledge, but the acquisition of flair in using that knowledge requires a certain talent, particularly with words. Lately there have been percolating into the boardroom a considerable number of words which were coined for special purposes and grouped for new meanings or for effect or even for use in the game of intellectual one-upmanship. The value of this specialized language lies in its capacity to change as the society around us changes. Certainly the old words are inadequate to explain complicated new activities and concepts. To convey new concepts we need new words. Whether these new words—these buzzwords—will flourish or die, at least for a time they serve as a means of rapid, effective communication within the overall directorate and management system.

Bombarded with new words.

One of the key dimensions of boardroom activity is communication. The board chairman's leadership role requires that he react intelligently to the impact of specialized words that bombard him from management scientists and business whiz-kids inside the organization. At the same time the chairman and directors are bombarded with new words from the outside world of government, politics, science and technology, and sociology.

As the issues facing boards become increasingly complex, directors have to develop a new attitude and, along with it, a new vocabulary in order to deal with the multiplicity of contemporary pressures. The thrust of language innovation within the boardroom is toward a vocabulary that will sharpen communication. The precursor words are already there in the fields of technology, economics, and political and social science; they are invading the boardroom in the form of *boardspeak*. Not a small part of the director's challenge is to continually improve his ability to communicate within the boardroom and, as required, with the staff as well as to understand the staff. Most innovation in business language comes up from management rather than down from the board. Because new concepts are generally expressed in buzzwords, the director needs to learn at least some of these in order to understand the managers and fellow directors who may be a flair ahead of him in verbalistics.

Paradoxically, buzzwords serve both to confuse and to enlighten, depending upon which end of the dialog you are on. However, it is unrealistic and unsatisfactory to ignore the development of new phrases and new words just because a specialized vocabulary is outside one's own field of activity.

There is a fun aspect to buzzwords, and this has its own value in the boardroom—which is not known as a particularly humorous environment. Sometimes buzzwords can lighten the subject at hand, but their primary purpose is to transmit in shortened form a new concept, a new idea, a new reference point that is useful in conducting the board's activities. At the same time there must be discrimination and discard of the flash phrases and buzzwords created only for effect and not for transmission of a new idea.

What Is a Buzzword?

Years ago William James described the world of a baby's earliest observation as presenting to the baby "one big blooming, buzzing confusion." Long after, the late Professor Ralph Hower of Harvard Business School was given credit for providing the label *buzzwords* for phrases that buzz pleasantly in our ears and roll easily off our tongues. It has been said that the staying power of Elton Mayo's buzzwords lay in their special meanings for listening, emotional release, upward communication, and social skills. Because of these meanings, Mayo's words have become part of the everyday vocabulary of managers and directors alike. Planning words (diversification, synergy); computer words (systems analysis, management information systems); social science words (affluent society, hard-core, life style)—all have made the grade from the buzzword stage to the accepted vocabulary of the executive suite and the boardroom.

World War II, with its operations research development, added dramatic phrases: model building, econometric models, input–output statistics, programming, turnaround documents, heuristics. This was followed by the computer era, which continues to add buzzwords almost daily. The mortality rate of buzzwords is high, but the director is justified in staying tuned in, because they are usually the precursors of useful change.

We cannot neglect the multitude of government activities that are becoming more sophisticated and complicated as well as more bureaucratic. Endless buzzwords pour out of the Defense Department, NASA, the General Accounting Office, the FBI.

Whittaker Corporation's director and former president William M. Duke is a phrasemaker who was a favorite of journalists during the time when his far-flung conglomerate was particularly profitable. Dr. Duke, a scientist turned manager, was quite eloquent about management and sprinkled his interviews with such terms as macroscopic insights, monotonic earnings growth, and product repeatability. When securities analysts asked insistently why Whittaker has to keep pushing onward and upward, Dr. Duke had a simple explanation: "No growth is nugatory to shareholder values." Despite the analysts' raised eyebrows, Dr.

Duke's rhetoric brought fresh insights and pizzazz to the directorate and management world.

Dr. James B. Conant insisted back in the early sixties that a first step to reform is to call a thing by its right name, without upholstering. Specifically, Dr. Conant asserted that you can't wipe out a slum until you are ready to call it a slum. On a larger scale, the persistent growth of euphemism in a language may distort thought and forestall action, since its fundamental intent is to deceive. "Pacification of the enemy infrastructure" sounded so plausible and innocuous that most people readily accepted it, yet they might have reacted differently had the military said it was blasting the Viet Cong out of a village.

Euphemisms are not confined to the professions or the military or high society; the garbagemen of Milwaukee, Wisconsin, recently petitioned the city for a change in title; they asked to be called public works combustible field men. No doubt the recent ecology kick had something to do with this desire to become "pollutical scientists."

Wordmanship

Sir Winston Churchill, Dr. Samuel Johnson, the Madison Avenue superstars of wordmanship—each has helped embroider and influence the word world of the executive and the direc-

The persistent growth of euphemism may distort thought
and forestall action.

tor. But not all practitioners of wordmanship are equally skilled, and without skill we may confuse rather than communicate. Unless new words can make a positive contribution to the boardroom and to management understanding, they should be abandoned in favor of more familiar terminology. Yet, buzzwords do persist, and any buzzword selection will be dynamic and controversial by its very nature.

In the spring of 1971 more than 350 directors and top managers from Britain and continental Europe heard Dr. Igor Ansof say that the information used by large corporations to guide decisions is historic, hierarchical, one-way. The director of a large corporation more recently complained to Dr. Ansof that he was no longer able to understand 80 percent of the things his managers told him. In reply Dr. Ansof said, "We are driving our business through looking into the rear-view mirror," which works well only so long as the road ahead is straight.

It is difficult to find straightforward communication in the boardroom or in government affairs because an excess of ill-chosen buzzwords pervades the language and the system. These words become part of the jargon—officialese, journalese, commercialese, economese, even a reverse gobbledegook of short, terse, shirtsleeve English, which is in part a revulsion against other forms of gobbledegook. It is noteworthy that President Nixon's speechwriters sought to screen bureaucratic jargon out of his first-term messages and speeches and have banned a number of words, including viable, parameter, hegemony, and dichotomy.

The promotional literature on new life styles and games people play indicates that when two people communicate, 93 percent of the total message is transmitted in a nonverbal way and only 7 percent is conveyed by words. Most of us, however, have been educated to rely on words for communication and are unaware of the ways in which the body telegraphs emotion.

As the director goes about his affairs he learns to recognize the various forms of buzzwords: (1) those that are associated with certain advanced management concepts, principles, and theory at one point in time, including venerable theories yet to be reduced to practice; (2) those that are the more expressive terms from specialist areas within management (marketing, finance, long-range planning, personnel) and are replacing classical terms and reflecting the dynamism of advancing concepts and theories; and (3) those that are not so broadly known technical terms derived from management techniques such as operations research, merger and acquisition practice, investment and securities analysis, and production and statistical quality control. Too, some buzzwords are just interesting words and phrases from peripheral subject areas such as law, mathematics, behavioral and social sciences, economics, and political science which could have an impact in the boardroom.

Like street slang, buzzwords come and go suddenly, mysteriously. The best of them remain to enlarge and perhaps enrich the language. Our vocabulary is replete with terms that were once the buzzwords of new fields: aviation, aerospace, mass communications, data processing. Sometimes new words are coined (aerospace), sometimes old words are given new meanings (broadcast), sometimes buzzwords are merely pollutants that muddy our communication waters. But whatever their shape, and whatever their source, and whatever their duration, buzzwords can help to make the boardroom hum.

Notes

PREFACE

[page viii]   The words of James Russell Lowell are quoted from *New England: Two Centuries Ago.*

CHAPTER 1

[page 1]   The opening quotation is from an unknown source.

[page 4]   Robert Heller's comment about board dominance appears in *The Great Executive Dream* (New York: Delacorte Press, 1972).

[page 6]   The report of the Land study is paraphrased (by permission of the author) from *Building a More Effective Board of Directors.* The study was made by Harry Rex Land, Jr., H. R. Land & Company, Los Angeles, California (undated).

CHAPTER 2

[page 12]   The opening quotation is from the London *Daily News* of October 25, 1877.

[page 18]   The quotation on stewardship and time comes from 1684 Norris Poems. *A New English Dictionary* (Oxford, 1897), p. 46.

[page 22]   The reference to ginger groups appeared in the September 1972 issue of *The Director.*

CHAPTER 3

[page 24]   The opening quotation is taken from Edmund Burke's treatise, *Reflections on the French Revolution,* published in 1790.

[page 27]   The article by Desfosses and Smith, "Corporate Directors Under Fire," appeared in *California Management Review,* Winter 1973, pp. 91–97.

[page 28]   The biblical quotation on diligence comes from Proverbs 22:29.

[page 28]   The Shakespearean quotation on diligence is from *King Lear* (I:v).

[page 29]   The case of *Litwin* v. *Allen* is reported in 25 N.Y.S. 2d, 667 (1940). Justice Shientag's words are found on page 685.

[page 30]   The case of *Bayer* v. *Beran* is reported in 49 N.Y.S. 2d, 2 (1944). Justice Shientag's words are to be found on page 5.

[page 35]   The case of *Meinhard* v. *Salmon* is reported in 249 N.Y. 458, 164 N.E. 545 (1928). Justice Cardozo's words appear on page 546.

CHAPTER 4

[page 36]   The opening quotation is from G. K. Chesterton.

[page 37]   Mark Spade, *How to Run a Bassoon Factory* and *Business for Pleasure* (London: Hamish Hamilton, 1950).

[page 40]   Lynn A. Brau's study of directors in the United States and Europe was reported in *The Director*, November 1969.

[page 47]   The quotation on the director as watchdog is taken from L. J. Bowen in re: North Australian Territory Co. (1892), 1 ch. 322, 341.

[page 47]   H. F. Tecoz's personal survey was reported in *Business Week*, September 16, 1972.

[page 52]   *German International*, an independent English-language monthly news magazine published in Bonn-Lengsdorf, has kindly given permission to quote the "Letter to a Foreign Business Man" from its February 1973 issue.

[page 55]   The answers to "Why a board of directors?" appear in J. M. Juran and J. Keith Louden, *The Corporate Director* (New York: AMA, 1966).

[page 55]   The case of *Manson* v. *Curtis* is reported in 223 N.Y. 313, 323.

CHAPTER 5

[page 56]   The opening quotation is from Junius, City Address and the King's Answer, Letter 37, published in 1770.

[page 58]   Dr. Vance's analysis of board types is to be found in *The Corporate Director: A Critical Evaluation* (Homewood, Ill.: Dow Jones–Irwin, Inc., 1968).

[page 60]   The British Institute of Management published the findings of its study in its Management Survey Report No. 10 (1972).

[page 65]   Voltaire's words are quoted from *Candide*, published in 1759.

[page 68]   The closing quotation is from La Rochefoucauld.

CHAPTER 6

[page 69]   The opening quotation is from Lord Boothby's caricature of the life of a director in England.

[page 70]   The quotation on the functions of a director is from the *Bulletin of Ordinance*, as reprinted in *The Director*, June 1969.

[page 72]   Stafford Beer's extended analogy appears in *Brain of the Firm* (London: The Penguin Press, 1972).

[page 79]   For more on the Zuñi Indians, see Ruth Benedict, *Patterns of Culture* (Boston: Houghton Mifflin, 1934).

[page 79]   For more on the Karimojong, see Lucy Mair, *Primitive Government* (Gloucester, Mass.: Peter Smith, n.d.).

[page 80]   The closing quotation is from William Bolitho's *Twelve Against the Gods*. See *The Home Book of Quotations*, Burton Stevenson, ed. (New York: Dodd, Mead, 1967.)

CHAPTER 7
[page 81]   The opening quotation appears in Leslie Coulthard, *The Director*, August 1966.

[page 84]   For more on Japanese compensation plans, see T. F. M. Adams and N. Kobayashi, *The World of Japanese Business* (Tokyo: Kodansha International, Ltd., 1969).

[page 86]   For the details of Washington's methods of expense accounting, see Marvin Kitman, *George Washington's Expense Account* (New York: Simon & Schuster, 1970).

[page 86]   For more on the Kienbaum study, see "Perks for the Boys," *German International*, April 1972, pp. 30–32.

[page 92]   The closing quotation is from Alexander Pope's *Moral Essays*, Epistle iii.

CHAPTER 8
[page 94]   Stafford Beer's book is *Brain of the Firm* (London: The Penguin Press, 1972).

[page 94]   Mark Spade's characterization can be found in *How to Run a Bassoon Factory* (London: Hamish Hamilton, 1950).

[page 95]   Martin Page writes about the AGM in *The Company Savage* (London: Cassell, 1972).

CHAPTER 9
[page 112]   The wry bit of doggerel on the board secretary is from *Standard Boardroom Practice* (London: Institute of Directors, revised 1971), pp. 52–53.

[page 113]   Great Britain's Companies Act became law in 1948. The section on the registration of minutes is 145 (2).

CHAPTER 10
[page 117]   The opening quotation is from Sydney Smith, as quoted in *Dangers and Advantages of Wit*.

[page 122]   The study of humor and teaching skill was reported in *School & Society*, Vol. 24, September 25, 1926.

[page 123]   Enid Welsford's study of the jester is *The Fool, His Social and Literary History* (Gloucester, Mass.: Peter Smith, 1966; first published by Faber and Faber, Ltd., in London in 1935).

[page 127]   Albert Rapp's story of Amasis can be found in *The Origins of Wit and Humor* (New York: Dutton, 1951).

CHAPTER 11
[page 129]   The opening quotation is from Plato's *Diogenes Laertius*.

[page 131]   For more of Graham Claverley's theory, see *Managers and Magic* (London: Longman Group Ltd., 1971).

[page 132]   Adams's law is from J. Stacy Adams, "Inequity in Social Exchange," in L. Berkowitz (ed.), *Advances in Experimental Social Psychology* (New York: Academic Press, 1965).

[page 133]   For more on Ashby's law see W. Ross Ashby, *Design for a Brain* (London: Chapman & Hall, 1952).

[page 133]   Astor's laws appeared in *Boardroom Reports,* Vol. 1, No. 2, May 8, 1972.

[page 133]   Beer's theorem was published in *Brain of the Firm* (London: The Penguin Press, 1972).

[page 134]   Bennis's laws appear in his *The Leaning Ivory Tower* (San Francisco: Jossey-Bass, 1973).

[page 134]   Bright's law, or proposition, as he prefers to call it, is the brainchild of Professor James R. Bright, formerly of Harvard Business School and now of the University of Texas. For his landmark work see *Research, Development, and Technological Innovations* (Homewood, Ill.: Richard D. Irwin, 1964).

[page 135]   Hurley Cook, the author of Cook's law, is associate editor of *Chemical Bulletin,* which published his propeon ratio in March 1972.

[page 136]   For more on Copeman's principle see his *The Chief Executive and Business Growth,* a comparative study of the United States, Britain, and Germany (London and New York: Leviathan House, 1971).

[page 137]   Crosby's laws are taken from *The Art of Getting Your Own Sweet Way* (New York: McGraw-Hill, 1972) and are used with permission of McGraw-Hill Book Company.

[page 140]   For more on Fyffe's axiom see *Dun's Review,* August 1973.

[page 140]   GG's law is propounded by Guy Goden in "The G Constant," *The Journal of Irreproducible Results,* March 1972.

[page 141]   Greenberg's first law of expertise appeared in *Saturday Review Science* on November 25, 1972.

[page 142]   Gumperson's law is reproduced courtesy of Robert Miss of the American College Public Relations Committee.

[page 142]   Heller's truths of management are from Robert Heller, *The Great Executive Dream* (New York: Delacorte, 1972). Copyright © 1972 by Robert Heller and reprinted by permission of Delacorte Press.

[page 143]   For more about making confusion into an understandable phenomenon, see L. Ron Hubbard, *The Problems of Work: Scientology Applied to the Work-a-Day World* (Los Angeles: American Saint Hill Organization, Church of Scientology, 1956).

[page 144]   Hull's law appears in Laurence F. Peter and Raymond Hull, *The Peter Principle* (New York: William Morrow, 1969).

[page 144]   For more on Hymer's laws see *Transnational Relations and World Politics,* Robert O. Keohane and Joseph S. Nye, Jr. (eds.) (Cambridge, Mass.: Harvard University Press, 1972), p. 51.

[page 145]   James's law is cited in Denis James, *Bluff Your Way in Management* (London: Wolfe Publishing, 1969).

[page 145]   Julian's law is discussed in Daniel Dash, "A Code of Many Colors, Ethics in International Engineering," *Worldwide P&I Planning,* March/April 1972.

[page 145]   Mr. Kemmer is general manager of the patent and license division of Standard Oil Company (Ohio). For more on his law see *Les Nouvelles,* the journal of the Licensing Executives' Society, September 1972.

[page 146]   For more on Lane Tracy's laws see his "Postscript to the Peter Principle," *Harvard Business Review,* July–August 1972.

[page 146]   Mason Haire's law of the situation was set forth in his *Organization Theory in Industrial Practice* (New York: Wiley, 1962), pp. 7–8.

[page 147]   Mauss's law is cited in Martin Page, *The Company Savage* (London: Cassell, 1972).

[page 147]   Meyer's laws were published in *Marketing/Communications* of August 1970.

[page 148]   For a partly humorous application of Murphy's law see C. M. Venegas, "Murphy's Law and a Liquid Helium Bath Temperature Controller," *The Journal of Irreproducible Results,* December 1970.

[page 150]   Paddy O'Neil-Dunne's rules are to be found in "Across the Board by Gulliver (Ten Rules for Business Gamblers)," *The Director,* February 1972.

[page 151]   Page's law is expanded on in *The Company Savage* (London: Cassell, 1972).

[page 151]   For more on Parkinson's laws see *Parkinson's Law* (Boston: Houghton Mifflin, 1957); *The Law and the Profits* (Boston: Houghton Mifflin, 1960); *In-Laws and Outlaws* (Boston: Houghton Mifflin, 1962); and *The Law of Delay: Interviews and Outerviews* (London: John Murray, 1970).

[page 152]   For a complete exposition of the Peter principle see Laurence F. Peter and Raymond Hull, *The Peter Principle* (New York: William Morrow, 1969).

[page 152]   Piet Hein's first law of budgeting can be found in Piet Hein, *Still More Grooks,* published in Copenhagen by Borgans Forlag and in Garden City, New York, by Doubleday in 1970.

[page 152]   The Pinocchio principle is detailed in Kenneth E. Boulding, *Challenge to Leadership* (New York: Free Press, 1973).

[page 153]   For more on Snow's law see C. P. Snow, *Science and Government,* the Godkin Lectures at Harvard University, 1960, p. 118. © by the President and Fellows of Harvard College.

[page 154]   Trowbridge's laws are reprinted by special permission from the September 1972 issue of *International Management.* Copyright © by McGraw-Hill International Publications Company Limited. All rights reserved.

[page 155]   Weil's law is quoted from *The New York Times* of March 2, 1973.

CHAPTER **12**
[page 156]   The opening quotation is from Clarence C. Walton, *Ethos and the Executive* (Englewood Cliffs, N.J.: Prentice-Hall, 1969).

CHAPTER **13**
[page 169]   For a more complete treatment of buzzwords see Robert Kirk Mueller, *Buzzwords: A Guide to the New Language of Leadership* (New York: Van Nostrand Reinhold, 1974).

Selected
Bibliography

Bacon, Jeremy. *Corporate Directorship Practices,* Business Policy Study 125. A Joint Report from National Industrial Conference Board and American Society of Corporate Secretaries, New York, 1967. 162 pp.

————. *Corporate Directorship Practices: Membership and Committees of the Board,* Conference Board Report 588. A Joint Research Report from The Conference Board and American Society of Corporate Secretaries. © 1973 The Conference Board, Inc., New York.

Baker, J. C. *Directors and Their Functions.* Boston: Harvard University Graduate School of Business Administration, 1945.

The Board of Directors: New Challenges, New Directions. New York: The Conference Board, 1972. 73 pp.

The Board of Directors—A Survey of Its Structure, Composition, and Role. Management Survey Report 10. London: British Institute of Management, 1972.

Brown, C. C., and Smith, E. E. *The Director Looks at His Job.* New York: Columbia University Press, 1957.

Bull, George. *The Director's Handbook.* Maidenhead, Berkshire, England: McGraw-Hill, 1969. 832 pp.

Copeland, M. T., and Towl, A. R. *The Board of Directors and Business Management.* Boston: Harvard Business School, 1947. 194 pp.

The Corporate Director and the Investing Public. New York Stock Exchange, 1962. 47 pp.

Corporate Directorship Practices. Supplementary Notes: 1971. New York: American Society of Corporate Secretaries (One Rockefeller Plaza). 97 pp.

Davis, William, and Friedman, Edith J. *Corporate Secretary's Encyclopedia,* Vols. I–IV. Englewood Cliffs, N.J.: Prentice-Hall, 1958.

Expenses and Benefits. London: Institute of Directors, 1954. 21 pp.

Feuer, Mortimer. *Handbook for Corporate Directors.* Englewood Cliffs, N.J.: Prentice-Hall, 1961.

Financial and Accounting Responsibilities of Directors. London: The General Educational Trust of the Institute of Chartered Accountants in England and Wales (Moorgate Place), 1970. 23 pp.

Foster, Eric, and Bull, George, eds. *The Director, His Money and His Job.* Maidenhead, Berkshire, England: McGraw-Hill, 1970. 398 pp.

Jackson, Percival E. *What Every Corporation Director Should Know.* New York: William-Frederick Press, 1949. 183 pp.

Juran, J. M., and Louden, J. K. *The Corporate Director.* New York: AMA, 1966. 388 pp.

Kinley, John R. *Corporate Directorship Practices.* New York: The Conference Board, 1972.

Koontz, Harold. *The Board of Directors and Effective Management.* New York: McGraw-Hill, 1957. 268 pp.

Lock, Dennis, and Tavernier, Gerard, eds. *Director's Guide to Management Techniques.* London: Director's Bookshelf, imprinted jointly by Institute of Directors and Gower Press, 1970. 442 pp.

Mace, Myles L. *The Board of Directors in Small Corporations.* Boston: Harvard Business School, 1948. 92 pp.

———. *Directors—Myth and Reality.* Boston: Harvard Business School, 1972. 207 pp.

Miller, B. *Manual and Guide for the Corporate Secretary,* Vols. I–III. Englewood Cliffs, N.J.: Prentice-Hall, 1969.

Nicholson, Miklos S. *Duties and Liabilities of Corporate Officers and Directors.* Englewood Cliffs, N.J.: Prentice-Hall, 1972. 345 pp.

Parker, Hugh, et al. *Effective Board Room Management.* London: British Institute of Management, 1971.

Puckey, Sir Walter. *The Board Room.* London: Hutchinson, 1969.

———. *Management Principles,* 2d rev. ed. London: Hutchinson, 1970. 179 pp.

Read, Alfred. *The Company Director, His Functions, Powers and Duties.* Prepared under the authority of the Council of the Institute of Directors. 4th ed. London: Jordàn & Sons, 1971. 232 pp.

Shenfield, Barbara. *Company Boards, Their Responsibilities to Shareholders, Employees, and the Community.* London: George Allen & Unwin, 1971. 175 pp.

Thompson, G. C., and Walsh, F. J. "Directors' Compensation, Fringe Benefits and Retirement," *Conference Board Record,* February 1965.

Vance, Stanley C. *Boards of Directors, Structure and Performance.* Eugene: University of Oregon, 1964.

———. *The Corporate Director: A Critical Evaluation.* Homewood, Ill.: Dow Jones–Irwin, 1968.

Index